INANNA
QUEEN OF HEAVEN AND EARTH

INANNA
QUEEN OF HEAVEN AND EARTH

Her Stories and Hymns from Sumer

DIANE WOLKSTEIN
and
SAMUEL NOAH KRAMER

Art compiled by Elizabeth Williams-Forte

1817

HARPER & ROW, PUBLISHERS, New York
Cambridge, Philadelphia, San Francisco,
London, Mexico City, São Paulo, Sydney

INANNA: QUEEN OF HEAVEN AND EARTH. Copyright © 1983 by Diane Wolkstein and Samuel Noah Kramer. All rights reserved. Printed in the United States of America. No part of this book may be used or reproduced in any manner whatsoever without written permission except in the case of brief quotations embodied in critical articles and reviews. For information address Harper & Row, Publishers, Inc., 10 East 53rd Street, New York, N.Y. 10022. Published simultaneously in Canada by Fitzhenry & Whiteside Limited, Toronto.

FIRST EDITION

Designer: C. Linda Dingler

Library of Congress Cataloging in Publication Data

Wolkstein, Diane.
    Inanna, queen of heaven and earth.

    Translation and retelling of the Inanna
stories from the Sumerian.
        Bibliography: p.
        Includes index.
        I. Inanna (Sumerian deity) 2. Mythology,
Sumerian. 3. Inanna (Sumerian deity)—Poetry.
I. Kramer, Samuel Noah, 1897– II. Title.
BL1616.15W64   1983   299'.92   80–8690
ISBN 0–06–014713–X
ISBN 0–06–090854–8 (pbk.)

83 84 85 86 87 10 9 8 7 6 5 4 3 2 1
04 05   40 39 38 37 36 35 34 33 32

For my daughter, Rachel Cloudstone Zucker

CONTENTS

Commentaries

INANNA'S FAMILY TREE

The stories in this cycle express an amalgamation of Sumerian and Akkadian religious and political beliefs that go back at least a thousand years before Sumer was a unified political entity. During the third millennium B.C., there were periodic attempts to unify the various city-states in Sumer and Akkad; and with the increasing political centralization came a concurrent movement to bring together the many local gods and goddesses into one pantheon.

In the Cycle of Inanna, we encounter aspects of the earlier Sumerian Dumuzi as well as the later more politicized Akkadian Dumuzi. The Sumerian Dumuzi, who comes from the agricultural, more traditional area of southern Sumer, Eridu, which emphasized order (the *me*), is characterized as the force in the grain and as the priestly lover and attendant of the Fertility Goddess, Inanna. The Akkadian Dumuzi, coming from the northern nomadic peoples who emphasized the arbitrary will and power of the gods, is characterized as the shepherd, the astral heavenly bull, and the king who has "godlike" powers. Inanna, too, by her epithet Queen of Heaven and Earth, subsumed the many local cults to the goddess and combined the earlier, more peaceful Fertility Goddess with the attributes of the more directing and directive Goddess of Love.

Although in other legends and stories the Sumerian divinities and heroes may have different relationships to each other, for the purpose of clarification the family tree on the following page indicates the relationships of the divinities to each other within the context of these stories.

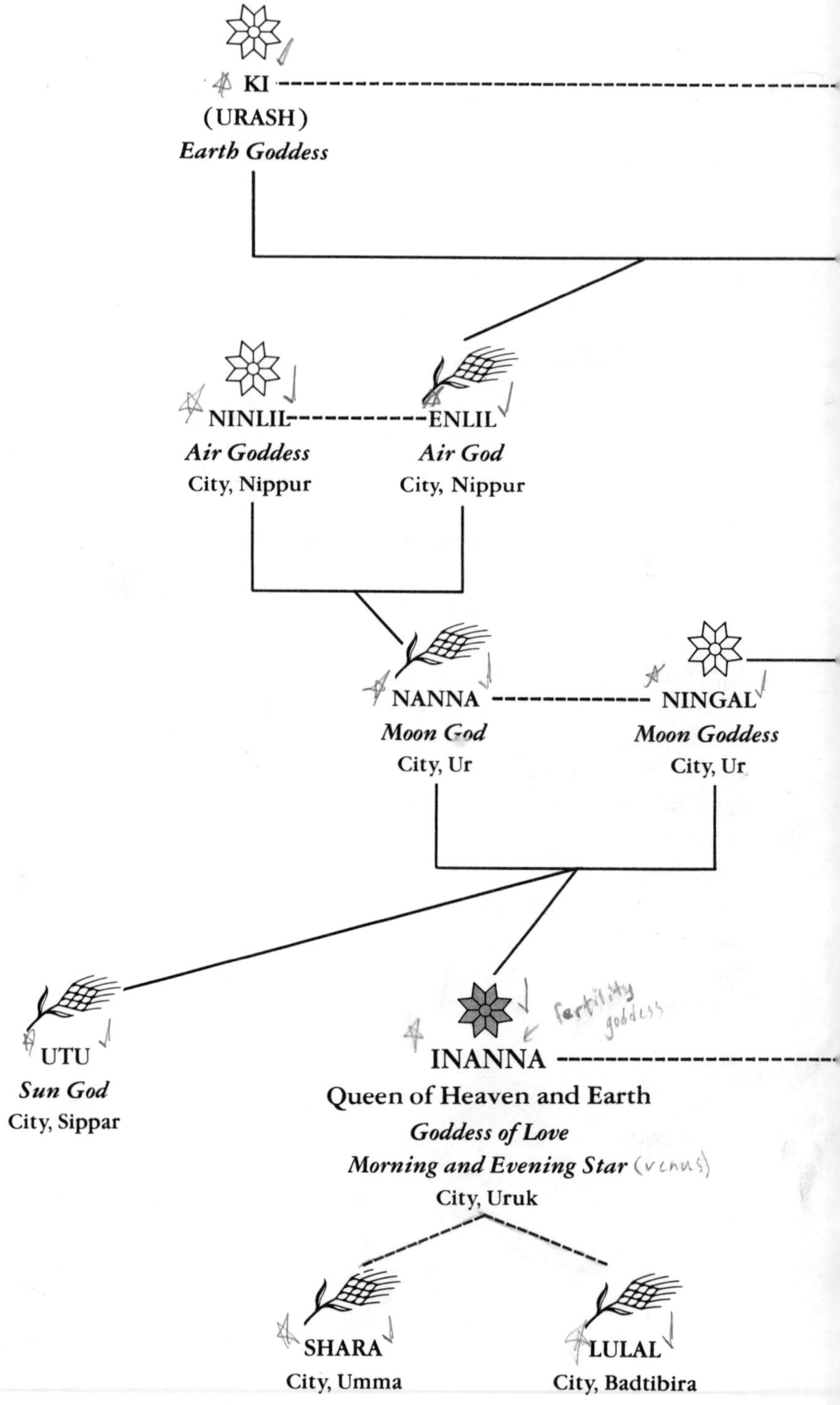

KI
(URASH)
Earth Goddess

NINLIL----------ENLIL
Air Goddess   *Air God*
City, Nippur   City, Nippur

NANNA - - - - - - - - - - NINGAL
Moon God   *Moon Goddess*
City, Ur   City, Ur

UTU
Sun God
City, Sippar

INANNA
fertility goddess
Queen of Heaven and Earth
Goddess of Love
Morning and Evening Star (venus)
City, Uruk

SHARA   LULAL
City, Umma   City, Badtibira

INANNA'S FAMILY TREE

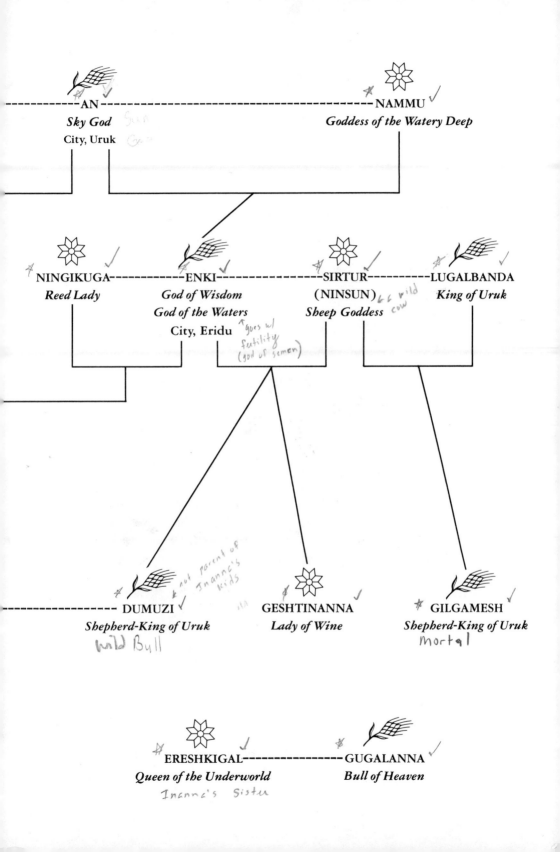

AN — *Sky God* — City, Uruk   **NAMMU** — *Goddess of the Watery Deep*

NINGIKUGA — *Reed Lady*   **ENKI** — *God of Wisdom, God of the Waters*, City, Eridu   **SIRTUR (NINSUN)** — *Sheep Goddess*   **LUGALBANDA** — *King of Uruk*

DUMUZI — *Shepherd-King of Uruk*   **GESHTINANNA** — *Lady of Wine*   **GILGAMESH** — *Shepherd-King of Uruk*

ERESHKIGAL — *Queen of the Underworld*   **GUGALANNA** — *Bull of Heaven*

Handwritten annotations: Sun, Cyn[?] (by AN); ✓ (by NAMMU); ✓ (by NINGIKUGA); ✓ (by ENKI); "goes w/ fertility (god of semen)" (by ENKI); ✓, "wild cow" (by SIRTUR/NINSUN); ✓ (by LUGALBANDA); "not parent of Inanna's kids", ✓ (by DUMUZI); "Wild Bull" (below DUMUZI); ✓ (by GESHTINANNA); ✓, "Mortal" (by GILGAMESH); ✓ (by ERESHKIGAL); "Inanna's Sister" (below ERESHKIGAL); ✓ (by GUGALANNA)

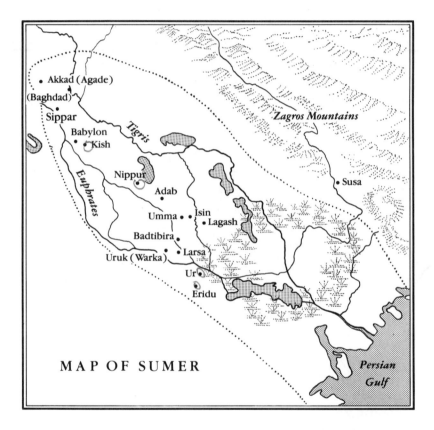

Akkad (Agade)

(Baghdad)

Sippar

Babylon

Kish

Tigris

Euphrates

Nippur

Adab

Umma

Isin

Lagash

Badtibira

Larsa

Uruk (Warka)

Ur

Eridu

Zagros Mountains

Susa

Persian Gulf

MAP OF SUMER

PREFACE

by Samuel Noah Kramer

This book is a graphic example of an effective cooperation between two specialists working in contrasting, yet complementary, areas of humanistic research: a folklorist who has collected and recorded the tales, legends, and songs of modern contemporary societies, and a cuneiformist who has devoted his entire scholarly career to the restoration and translation of the written tales, legends, and songs of the ancient Sumerians.

The Sumerian tales, legends, and songs are part of a vast literature inscribed on clay tablets and fragments scattered throughout museums the world over. Their contents, which date back to 2000 B.C., are now in the process of being deciphered, translated, and interpreted by a small international group of dedicated scholars; gradually, they are becoming available in one form or another to the world at large. Inscribed on these tablets and fragments, numbering some five to six thousand in all, are hundreds of compositions—myths, epic tales, hymns, psalms, love songs, laments, essays, disputations, proverbs, fables—that constitute a treasure house of comparative source material for the historian of literature and religion, for the biblical and classical scholar, and (as this book demonstrates) for the folklorist and cultural anthropologist.

The main goal of the selection presented here is to provide the reader with an authentic portrait of Sumer's most beloved and revered deity, the goddess Inanna. To compile this collection, I first combed the extant Sumerian literary documents, which I had deciphered and translated over the decades, for the relevant compositions on Inanna. Then, with the help of the most recent contributions by fellow Sumerologists, I brought the translations up to date. Finally, I turned the stories over to Diane Wolkstein, who proceeded to arrange, combine, and mold their raw contents in a way that would make them alive and meaningful to modern readers.

As a gifted storyteller and professional folklorist, Diane Wolkstein performed her delicate task with originality, ingenuity, and sensitivity. She eliminated cluttering repetitions, added explanatory words and lines when advisable, restored a broken passage when possible, and skillfully wove the texts of numerous related poems into a unifying whole. Diane Wolkstein has succeeded in re-creating a significant group of rather esoteric tales and songs, long erased from the memory of man, in a form that is at once imaginative and evocative, attractive and engaging.

INTRODUCTION

by Diane Wolkstein

Inanna was a birthday gift—and more. In the spring of 1979 I had been asked by Priscilla Moulton to present a program at Simmons College in Boston the following November. As the date fell on the week of my birthday and the program was open to my choosing, I decided that this must be the occasion I had been waiting for.

I had for years wanted to tell the story of the Moon Goddess, Diana. Not only am I her namesake, but in her cyclical aspect, the Moon Goddess is an identifying symbol for women. And all of us, both women and men, have long needed a "grand" story of a woman—as inspiration, guide, and model—for ourselves as well as for our children.

To my surprise, four months of research on the moon goddesses of the world turned up only scattered bits. The most complete tale of the goddess is that of Demeter; but the story revolves around the mother-daughter aspect of the goddess, and I wanted to tell a story of the goddess in *all* her aspects. Where was she to be found?

To look at the statues of the goddess in museums and to read of her impact in books of mythology and religion was only a beginning. As a storyteller, in order to truly know her, I had to hear her speak. I had to find the goddess in relationship with others. In order to know her, I had to find her text.

I went through the world's anthologies in search of the names of moon goddesses: Ishtar, Mari, Diana, Isis, Hecate, Pasiphae, Selene, Brigit, Cybele, the Shekinah, Lilith, Persephone, Inanna . . . I sought her by name, and at last I found mention of her and her stories in Samuel Noah Kramer's most recent book, *From the Poetry of Sumer.* In this book, Kramer describes the goddess of the first civilization from which we have texts: "Female deities were worshipped and adored all through Sumerian history. . . . but the goddess who outweighed, overshadowed, and outlasted them all was a deity known to the Sumerians by the name of Inanna, 'Queen of Heaven,' and to the Semites who lived in Sumer by the name of Ishtar. Inanna played a greater role in myth, epic, and hymn than any other deity, male or female."[1]

[1]Samuel Noah Kramer, *From the Poetry of Sumer,* Berkeley: University of Berkeley Press, 1979, p. 71.

In Kramer's *The Sacred Marriage Rite*, [2] I found the various love poems of the young earthy Inanna and the story of the mature Inanna's descent into the underworld. I read Inanna's descent again and again. I was drawn to the story of the woman who gave up, at seven successive gates, all she had accomplished in life until she was stripped naked, with nothing remaining but her will to be reborn.

Although fragmented, the story of Inanna as I began to perceive it followed the same pattern as the archetypal Moon Goddess: the young woman who is courted; the ripe woman who enjoys her feminine powers and generously offers her bounty; and the mature woman who meets death in the underworld. In *The White Goddess,* Robert Graves conjectures on the heavenly aspect of the Triple Goddess, "As the Sky Goddess, she was the moon . . . as the New Moon or Spring she was girl; as the Full Moon or Summer she was woman; as the Old Moon or Winter she was hag. . . ."[3]

In Sumerian, Inanna's name means literally "Queen of Heaven," and she was called both the First Daughter of the Moon and the Morning and Evening Star (the planet Venus). In addition, in Sumerian mythology, she was known as the Queen of Heaven and Earth and was responsible for the growth of plants and animals and fertility in humankind. Then, because of her journey to the underworld, she took on the powers and mysteries of death and rebirth, emerging not only as a sky or moon goddess, but as the goddess who rules over the sky, the earth, and the underworld. Here was the goddess in *all* her aspects; here was my story.

But as I prepared the story for presentation, piecing together the different sections, there were many gaps and question marks in the text, often at the most crucial moments, and I wondered what many of the words meant— literally. My friend Susan Bergholz, long a Sumerianophile, suggested I telephone the source: Samuel Noah Kramer, who had deciphered the text.

"So you love Inanna?" Kramer said, answering the telephone himself. "Well, then come and see me." He was giving a Jayne Lecture on Inanna in two days' time at the Philosophical Society in Philadelphia and why didn't I come then?

I arrived eager and full of questions:

"In the first line of 'The Descent of Inanna,' 'From the Great Above she set her mind to the Great Below,' what exactly does 'mind' mean?"

"Ear," Kramer said.

"Ear?"

[2]Samuel Noah Kramer, *The Sacred Marriage Rite,* Bloomington, Indiana: University of Indiana Press, 1969.
[3]Robert Graves, *The White Goddess,* New York: Farrar, Straus, and Giroux, p. 386.

"Yes, the word for ear and wisdom in Sumerian are the same. But mind is what is meant."

"But—I could say 'ear'?"

"Well, you could."

"Is it *opened* her ear or *set* her ear?"

"Set. Set her ear, like a donkey that sets its ear at a particular sound."

As Kramer spoke, a shiver ran through me. When taken literally, the text itself announces the story's direction: From the Great Above the goddess opened (set) her ear, her receptor for wisdom, to the Great Below.

While these thoughts were darting about in my mind, Kramer looked at the shaping I had done of his texts and said that he thought if I could find a publisher there might be a possibility for our collaborating on a joint publication. I had read the story of "Inanna and the *Huluppu*-Tree," and asked Kramer if there were other stories about Inanna that were intact. He mentioned "Inanna and Enki: The Transfer of the Arts of Civilization from Eridu to Erech," but said it had not yet been completely translated into English.

In November of 1979 I told "The Courtship" and "The Descent of Inanna" at Simmons College to an astonished and awestruck audience. When I told Kramer about it, he insisted that the people were responding to me, but I assured him it was the Inanna who had captivated him for fifty years who was now captivating them as well. By February, 1980, we had an eager and supportive publisher. In March, Kramer sent me a translation of "The *Me.*" Then, a month later when Kramer showed me Reisman's scholarly translations of the hymns, I suddenly understood that with the rebirth of the goddess into the sky, the texts formed one story: the life story of the goddess, from her adolescence to her completed womanhood and "godship."

In beginning the work of trying to find the appropriate written form for the stories of Inanna, I tried prose, the form I knew best from storytelling. But I found myself continually returning to verse. After six months of experimenting with different forms for "The *Huluppu*-Tree," it seemed there was some invisible, irreducible essence buried in each Sumerian line. Only by keeping the actual Sumerian verse line could I hope to express the mystery and power that lay within it.

For over two years I worked on the texts Kramer gave me. On my visits to Kramer, I asked him: What did this word mean? This sentence? Could he express it in different English words? What did it mean literally in Sumerian? Sometimes he could answer my questions. Other times he'd throw up his hands and say: "No matter how many times you ask me the same question, I *still* don't know."

With Kramer's consent, I turned to the writings of Thorkild Jacobsen for alternative ideas and words. I consulted the translations of Kramer's students for further possibilities on puzzling sections. I condensed sections, added, and edited—always with the idea of "story" in mind. During the first year, I dreamed of being in an enormous green meadow and having the task of cleaning the meadow—blade by blade.

In thinking about the book, I felt it was essential to use the art of Sumer and the surrounding areas to illustrate the text. Elizabeth Williams-Forte offered me expert and encouraging guidance both in finding and in selecting the appropriate works of art. Together we spent many wonderful hours discussing and choosing the cylinder seals and terracotta sculptures that seemed best to express the stories' moods and meanings.

After the first nine months of reading everything I could find on Sumerian literature, culture, and history, speaking with Kramer, and working and reworking each line, I decided I had to bring the story once again to an audience. I arranged to tell the Cycle of Inanna at Robert Bly's Mother Goddess Conference in Maine in June, 1980. But the thought of telling the stories to other people propelled me to rework the text again. In fact, each time I have told Inanna I have reworked the text as I realized that expressions such as "days of yore" or "I, the Maid" would immediately deaden the receptivity of the audience.

Further changes came to the manuscript from the telling. Audiences had difficulty keeping more than one foreign name in their minds and at the same time following the flow of the story. For this reason I decided to use English epithets to accompany the names of the characters as they appear. I also tried to minimize the use of Sumerian place names and epithets. Still, I kept such Sumerian words as *kur, me, sukkal,* and *abzu,* for they are metaphysical concepts that seem to me intrinsic to Sumerian thought; and in time, I hope, they may come to enrich our English thought and language.

My aim has been to keep as close as possible to the power, wonder, and mystery embedded in the Sumerian texts, and simultaneously to render the stories both accessible and compelling. For the latter reason, I have eliminated much of the repetition. For the former reason, I have retained as much of the repetition and Sumerian grammatical structure as the flow of the story would allow (for example, the three-part progressing parallelism, as in he—father—Enki). Whenever there is a break in the text, I use ellipses. When a certain section seems to demand clarification, often because there is a break at a crucial point, parentheses have been used to indicate that these are my own words.

Here, then, is the Cycle of Inanna. In "The *Huluppu*-Tree," she appears to us as a young woman in search of her womanhood. In "Inanna and the God of Wisdom," she achieves her queenship. In "The Courtship of Inanna and Dumuzi," she chooses the shepherd Dumuzi to be her lover, her husband, and the King of Sumer. In "The Descent of Inanna," Inanna leaves for the underworld and is allowed to return from the Great Below only on the condition that she choose a substitute. In the last section of the cycle, the "Seven Hymns to Inanna," Inanna is greeted and loved in her many aspects.

The world's first love story, two thousand years older than the Bible— tender, erotic, shocking, and compassionate—is more than momentary entertainment. It is a sacred story that has the intention of bringing its audience to a new spiritual place. With Inanna, we enter the place of exploration: the place where not all energies have been tamed or ordered.

Inanna's scribe, Samuel Noah Kramer, gave me her words. I have sung them as best as I can. Now, we pass them on to you.

INANNA'S
STORIES AND HYMNS

THE *HULUPPU*-TREE

In the first days, in the very first days,
In the first nights, in the very first nights,
In the first years, in the very first years,

In the first days when everything needed was brought into being,
In the first days when everything needed was properly nourished,
When bread was baked in the shrines of the land,
And bread was tasted in the homes of the land,
When heaven had moved away from earth,
And earth had separated from heaven,
And the name of man was fixed;
When the Sky God, An, had carried off the heavens,
And the Air God, Enlil, had carried off the earth,
When the Queen of the Great Below, Ereshkigal, was given
    the underworld for her domain,

He set sail; the Father set sail,
Enki, the God of Wisdom, set sail for the underworld.
Small windstones were tossed up against him;
Large hailstones were hurled up against him;
Like onrushing turtles,
They charged the keel of Enki's boat.
The waters of the sea devoured the bow of his boat like wolves;
The waters of the sea struck the stern of his boat like lions.

At that time, a tree, a single tree, a *huluppu*-tree
Was planted by the banks of the Euphrates.
The tree was nurtured by the waters of the Euphrates.
The whirling South Wind arose, pulling at its roots
And ripping at its branches
Until the waters of the Euphrates carried it away.

A woman who walked in fear of the word of the Sky God, An,
Who walked in fear of the word of the Air God, Enlil,
Plucked the tree from the river and spoke:
    "I shall bring this tree to Uruk.
    I shall plant this tree in my holy garden."

Inanna cared for the tree with her hand.
She settled the earth around the tree with her foot.
She wondered:
    "How long will it be until I have a shining throne to sit upon?
    How long will it be until I have a shining bed to lie upon?"

The years passed; five years, then ten years.
The tree grew thick,
But its bark did not split.

Then a serpent who could not be charmed
Made its nest in the roots of the *huluppu*-tree.
The *Anzu*-bird set his young in the branches of the tree.
And the dark maid Lilith built her home in the trunk.

The young woman who loved to laugh wept.
How Inanna wept!
(Yet they would not leave her tree.)

As the birds began to sing at the coming of the dawn,
The Sun God, Utu, left his royal bedchamber.
Inanna called to her brother Utu, saying:
    "O Utu, in the days when the fates were decreed,
      When abundance overflowed in the land,
      When the Sky God took the heavens and the Air God the earth,
      When Ereshkigal was given the Great Below for her domain,
      The God of Wisdom, Father Enki, set sail for the underworld,
      And the underworld rose up and attacked him. . . .

At that time, a tree, a single tree, a *huluppu*-tree
Was planted by the banks of the Euphrates.
The South Wind pulled at its roots and ripped at its branches
Until the waters of the Euphrates carried it away.
I plucked the tree from the river;
  I brought it to my holy garden.
I tended the tree, waiting for my shining throne and bed.

Then a serpent who could not be charmed
Made its nest in the roots of the tree,

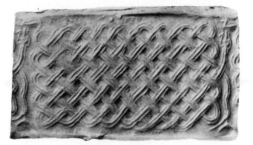

The *Anzu*-bird set his young in the branches of the tree,
And the dark maid Lilith built her home in the trunk.
I wept.
How I wept!
(Yet they would not leave my tree.)"

Utu, the valiant warrior, Utu,
Would not help his sister, Inanna.

As the birds began to sing at the coming of the second dawn,
Inanna called to her brother Gilgamesh, saying:
    "O Gilgamesh, in the days when the fates were decreed,
    When abundance overflowed in Sumer,
    When the Sky God had taken the heavens and the Air God
        the earth,

7

When Ereshkigal was given the Great Below for her domain,
The God of Wisdom, Father Enki, set sail for the underworld,
And the underworld rose up and attacked him.
At that time, a tree, a single tree, a *huluppu*-tree
Was planted by the banks of the Euphrates.
The South Wind pulled at its roots and ripped at its branches
Until the waters of the Euphrates carried it away.
I plucked the tree from the river;
  I brought it to my holy garden.
I tended the tree, waiting for my shining throne and bed.

Then a serpent who could not be charmed
Made its nest in the roots of the tree,

The *Anzu*-bird set his young in the branches of the tree,
And the dark maid Lilith built her home in the trunk.
I wept.
How I wept!
(Yet they would not leave my tree.)"

Gilgamesh the valiant warrior, Gilgamesh,
The hero of Uruk, stood by Inanna.

Gilgamesh fastened his armor of fifty minas around his chest.
The fifty minas weighed as little to him as fifty feathers.
He lifted his bronze ax, the ax of the road,
Weighing seven talents and seven minas, to his shoulder.
He entered Inanna's holy garden.

Gilgamesh struck the serpent who could not be charmed.
The *Anzu*-bird flew with his young to the mountains;
And Lilith smashed her home and fled to the wild, uninhabited places.
Gilgamesh then loosened the roots of the *huluppu*-tree;
And the sons of the city, who accompanied him, cut off the branches.

From the trunk of the tree he carved a throne for his holy sister.
From the trunk of the tree Gilgamesh carved a bed for Inanna.
From the roots of the tree she fashioned a *pukku* for her brother.
From the crown of the tree Inanna fashioned a *mikku* for Gilgamesh,
   the hero of Uruk.

INANNA AND THE
GOD OF WISDOM

Inanna placed the *shugurra,* the crown of the steppe, on her head.

She went to the sheepfold, to the shepherd.

She leaned back against the apple tree.

When she leaned against the apple tree, her vulva was wondrous to
behold.

Rejoicing at her wondrous vulva, the young woman Inanna applauded
herself.

She said:

"I, the Queen of Heaven, shall visit the God of Wisdom.

I shall go to the Abzu, the sacred place in Eridu.

I shall honor Enki, the God of Wisdom, in Eridu.

I shall utter a prayer to Enki at the deep sweet waters."

Inanna set out by herself.

When she was within a short distance of the Abzu,

He whose ears are wide open,

   He who knows the *me,* the holy laws of heaven and earth,

He who knows the heart of the gods,

Enki, the God of Wisdom, who knows all things,

Called to his servant, Isimud:

"Come, my *sukkal,*

The young woman is about to enter the Abzu.

When Inanna enters the holy shrine
Give her butter cake to eat.
Pour cold water to refresh her heart.
Offer her beer before the statue of the lion.
Treat her like an equal.
Greet Inanna at the holy table, the table of heaven."

presumably, altar inside the temple

Isimud heeded Enki's words.
When Inanna entered the Abzu,
He gave her butter cake to eat.
He poured cold water for her to drink.
He offered her beer before the statue of the lion.
He treated her respectfully.
He greeted Inanna at the holy table, the table of heaven.

13

Enki and Inanna drank beer together.

They drank more beer together.

They drank more and more beer together.

With their bronze vessels filled to overflowing,

With the vessels of Urash, Mother of the Earth,

They toasted each other; they challenged each other.

Enki, swaying with drink, toasted Inanna:

      "In the name of my power! In the name of my holy shrine!

      To my daughter Inanna I shall give

      The high priesthood! Godship!

      The noble, enduring crown! The throne of kingship!"

Inanna replied:

      "I take them!"

Enki raised his cup and toasted Inanna a second time:

      "In the name of my power! In the name of my holy shrine!

      To my daughter Inanna I shall give

Truth!
Descent into the underworld! Ascent from the underworld!
The art of lovemaking! The kissing of the phallus!"

Inanna replied:
"I take them!"

Enki raised his cup and toasted Inanna a third time:
"In the name of my power! In the name of my holy shrine!
To my daughter Inanna I shall give
The holy priestess of heaven!
The setting up of lamentations! The rejoicing of the heart!
The giving of judgments! The making of decisions!"

Inanna replied:
"I take them!"

(Fourteen times Enki raised his cup to Inanna.
Fourteen times he offered his daughter five *me*, six *me*, seven *me*.
Fourteen times Inanna accepted the holy *me*.)

Then Inanna, standing before her father, *not her real father.*
Acknowledged the *me* Enki had given to her:

"My father has given me the *me:*

He gave me the high priesthood.
He gave me godship.
He gave me the noble, enduring crown.
He gave me the throne of kingship.

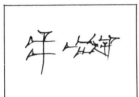

He gave me the noble sceptre.
He gave me the staff.
He gave me the holy measuring rod and line.
He gave me the high throne.
He gave me shepherdship.
He gave me kingship.

All have to do w/ ruling & power

He gave me the princess priestess.
He gave me the divine queen priestess.
He gave me the incantation priest.
He gave me the noble priest.
He gave me the libations priest.

a lot of clergy all w/ different responsibilities

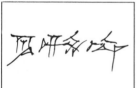

He gave me truth.
He gave me descent into the underworld.
He gave me ascent from the underworld.
He gave me the *kurgarra.*

gives her the power to go to & return from the under-world

He gave me the dagger and sword.
He gave me the black garment.
He gave me the colorful garment.
He gave me the loosening of the hair.
He gave me the binding of the hair.

symbols of power

16

He gave me the standard. ← holds banner (power in battle)

He gave me the quiver. ← holds arrows

He gave me the art of lovemaking.

He gave me the kissing of the phallus. ← oral sex

He gave me the art of prostitution.

He gave me the art of speeding.

He gave me the art of forthright speech.

He gave me the art of slanderous speech.

He gave me the art of adorning speech.

He gave me the cult prostitute.

He gave me the holy tavern.

He gave me the holy shrine.

He gave me the holy priestess of heaven.

He gave me the resounding musical instrument.

He gave me the art of song.

He gave me the art of the elder.

He gave me the art of the hero.

He gave me the art of power.

He gave me the art of treachery.

He gave me the art of straightforwardness.

He gave me the plundering of cities.

He gave me the setting up of lamentations.

He gave me the rejoicing of the heart.

He gave me deceit. ← lying works

He gave me the rebellious land.

He gave me the art of kindness.

He gave me travel.

He gave me the secure dwelling place.

17

He gave me the craft of the woodworker.
He gave me the craft of the copper worker.
He gave me the craft of the scribe.
He gave me the craft of the smith.
He gave me the craft of the leather maker.
He gave me the craft of the fuller. ← part of the process of weaving
He gave me the craft of the builder.
He gave me the craft of the reed worker. makes baskets

He gave me the perceptive ear.
He gave me the power of attention.
He gave me the holy purification rites.
He gave me the feeding pen.
He gave me the heaping up of hot coals. ← used for heat
He gave me the sheepfold.
He gave me fear.
He gave me consternation.
He gave me dismay.

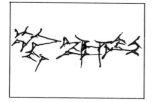

He gave me the bitter-toothed lion.
He gave me the kindling of fire.
He gave me the putting out of fire.
He gave me the weary arm.
He gave me the assembled family.
He gave me procreation.

He gave me the kindling of strife.
He gave me counseling.
He gave me heart-soothing.
He gave me the giving of judgments.
He gave me the making of decisions."

(Still reeling with drink) Enki spoke to his servant Isimud:

"My *sukkal,* Isimud—

The young woman—is about to leave—for Uruk.

It is my wish that she reach her city—safely."

Inanna gathered all the *me.*

The *me* were placed on the Boat of Heaven.

The Boat of Heaven, with the holy *me,* was pushed off from the quay.

When the beer had gone out from the one who had drunk beer,

When the beer had gone out from Father Enki,

When the beer had gone out from the great God of Wisdom,

Enki looked about the Abzu.

The eyes of the King of the Abzu searched Eridu.

King Enki looked about Eridu and called to his servant Isimud, saying:

"My *sukkal,* Isimud—"

"My king, Enki, I stand to serve you."

"The high priesthood? Godship?

The noble enduring crown?

Where are they?"

"My king has given them to his daughter."

"The art of the hero? The art of power?

Treachery? Deceit?

Where are they?"

"My king has given them to his daughter."

"The perceptive ear? The power of attention?
The making of decisions?
Where are they?"

"My king has given them to his daughter."

(Fourteen times Enki questioned his servant Isimud;
Fourteen times Isimud answered, saying:
"My king has given them to his daughter.
My king has given all the *me* to his daughter Inanna.")

Then Enki spoke, saying:
"Isimud, the Boat of Heaven, with the holy *me*
Where is it now?"

"The Boat of Heaven is (one quay away from Eridu)."

"Go! Take the *enkum*-creatures
Let them bring the Boat of Heaven back to Eridu!"

Isimud spoke to Inanna:
"My queen, your father has sent me to you.
Your father's words are words of state.
They may not be disobeyed."

Inanna answered:
"What has my father said?
What has Enki added?
What are his words of state that may not be disobeyed?"

Isimud spoke:

"My king has said:

'Let Inanna proceed to Uruk;

Bring the Boat of Heaven with the holy *me* back to Eridu.'"

Inanna cried:

"My father has changed his word to me!

He has violated his pledge—broken his promise!

Deceitfully my father spoke to me!

Deceitfully he cried:

'In the name of my power! In the name of my holy shrine!'

Deceitfully he sent you to me!"

Scarcely had Inanna spoken these words

When the wild-haired *enkum*-creatures seized the Boat of Heaven.

Inanna called to her servant Ninshubur, saying:

"Come, Ninshubur, once you were Queen of the East;

Now you are the faithful servant of the holy shrine of Uruk.

Water has not touched your hand,

Water has not touched your foot.

My *sukkal* who gives me wise advice,

My warrior who fights by my side,

Save the Boat of Heaven with the holy *me!*"

(Ninshubur sliced the air with her hand.

She uttered an earth-shattering cry.)

The *enkum*-creatures were sent hurtling back to Eridu.

Then Enki called to his servant Isimud a second time, saying:
   "My *sukkal,* Isimud—"

   "My king, Enki, I stand to serve you."

   "Where is the Boat of Heaven now?"

   "It is (two quays away from Eridu)."

   "Go! Take the fifty *uru*-giants,
      Let them carry off the Boat of Heaven."

The fifty flying *uru*-giants seized the Boat of Heaven.
But Ninshubur rescued the boat for Inanna.

Enki called to his servant Isimud a third time, saying:
   "My *sukkal,* Isimud—"

   "My king, Enki, I stand to serve you."

   "Where is the Boat of Heaven now?"

"It has just arrived at Dulma."

"Quickly! Take the fifty *lahama*-monsters,
  Let them carry off the Boat of Heaven."

The fifty *lahama*-sea monsters seized the Boat of Heaven.

But Ninshubur rescued the boat for Inanna.

A fourth time Enki sent the sound-piercing *kugalgal.* ← a monster

A fifth time Enki sent the *enunun.* a monster

But each time Ninshubur rescued the boat for Inanna.

Enki called to his servant Isimud a sixth time, saying:
  "My *sukkal,* Isimud—"

  "My king, Enki, I stand to serve you."

  "Where is the Boat of Heaven now?"

  "It is about to enter Uruk."

  "Quickly! Take the watchmen of the Iturungal Canal,
  Let them carry off the Boat of Heaven."

Isimud and the watchmen of the Iturungal Canal seized
  the Boat of Heaven,
But Ninshubur rescued the boat for Inanna.

Then Ninshubur spoke to Inanna:
      "My queen, when the Boat of Heaven
      Enters the Nigulla Gate of Uruk,
      Let high water flow in our city;
      Let the deep-going boats sail swiftly through our canals."

Inanna answered Ninshubur:
      "On the day the Boat of Heaven
      Enters the Nigulla Gate of Uruk,
      Let high water sweep over the streets;
      Let high water flow over the paths.
      Let the old men give counsel;
      Let the old women offer heart-soothing.
      Let the young men show the might of their weapons;
      Let the little children laugh and sing.
      Let all of Uruk be festive!
      Let the high priest greet the Boat of Heaven with song.
      Let him utter great prayers.
      Let the king slaughter oxen and sheep.
      Let him pour beer out of the cup.
      Let the drum and tambourine resound.
      Let the sweet *tigi-*music be played.
      Let all the lands proclaim my noble name.
      Let my people sing my praises."

And so it was,

On the day the Boat of Heaven entered the Nigulla Gate of Uruk,

High water swept over the streets;

High water flowed over the paths.

The Boat of Heaven docked at the holy shrine of Uruk;

The Boat of Heaven docked at the holy house of Inanna.

Then Enki called to his servant Isimud a seventh time, saying:

"My *sukkal,* Isimud—"

"My king, Enki, I stand to serve you."

"Where is the Boat of Heaven now?"

"The Boat of Heaven is at the White Quay." ← a stone dock / harbor

"Go! She has aroused wonder there.

The queen has aroused wonder at the White Quay.

Inanna has aroused wonder at the White Quay for

the Boat of Heaven."

The holy *me* were being unloaded.

As the *me* which Inanna had received from Enki were unloaded,

They were announced and presented to the people of Sumer.

Then more *me* appeared—more *me* than Enki had given Inanna.

And these, too, were announced,

And these, too, were presented to the people of Uruk:

"Inanna brought the *me:*

She brought the placing of the garment on the ground.

She brought allure.

She brought the art of women.

She brought the perfect execution of the *me.*

She brought the *tigi-* and *lilis-*drums.

She brought the *ub-,* the *meze-,* and the *ala-*tambourines. . . ."

Inanna spoke, saying:

"Where the Boat of Heaven has docked,

That place shall be called The White Quay.

Where the holy *me* have been presented,

That place I shall name The Lapis Lazuli Quay."

Then Enki spoke to Inanna, saying:

"In the name of my power! In the name of my holy shrine!
Let the *me* you have taken with you remain in the holy shrine
of your city.
Let the high priest spend his days at the holy shrine in song.
Let the citizens of your city prosper,
Let the children of Uruk rejoice.
The people of Uruk are allies of the people of Eridu.
Let the city of Uruk be restored to its great place."

THE COURTSHIP OF INANNA
AND DUMUZI

The brother spoke to his younger sister.
The Sun God, Utu, spoke to Inanna, saying:

"Young Lady, the flax in its fullness is lovely.
Inanna, the grain is glistening in the furrow.
I will hoe it for you. I will bring it to you.
A piece of linen, big or small, is always needed.
Inanna, I will bring it to you."

"Brother, after you've brought me the flax,
Who will comb it for me?"

"Sister, I will bring it to you combed."

"Utu, after you've brought it to me combed,
  Who will spin it for me?"

"Inanna, I will bring it to you spun."

"Brother, after you've brought the flax to me spun,
  Who will braid it for me?"

"Sister, I will bring it to you braided."

"Utu, after you've brought it to me braided,
  Who will warp it for me?"

"Inanna, I will bring it to you warped."

"Brother, after you've brought the flax to me warped,
  Who will weave it for me?"

"Sister, I will bring it to you woven."

"Utu, after you've brought it to me woven,
  Who will bleach it for me?"

"Inanna, I will bring it to you bleached."

"Brother, after you've brought my bridal sheet to me,
  Who will go to bed with me?
  Utu, who will go to bed with me?"

"Sister, your bridegroom will go to bed with you.
  He who was born from a fertile womb, ← means he's mortal
  He who was conceived on the sacred marriage throne, ← marriage was practiced by
  Dumuzi, the shepherd! He will go to bed with you." this was written (by Inanna)

31

Inanna spoke:

    "No, brother!

    The man of my heart works the hoe.

    The farmer! He is the man of my heart!

    He gathers the grain into great heaps.

    He brings the grain regularly into my storehouses."

Utu spoke:

    "Sister, marry the shepherd.

    Why are you unwilling?

His cream is good; his milk is good.
Whatever he touches shines brightly.
Inanna, marry Dumuzi.

You who adorn yourself with the agate necklace of fertility,
Why are you unwilling?
Dumuzi will share his rich cream with you.
You who are meant to be the king's protector,
Why are you unwilling?"

Inanna spoke:

"The shepherd! I will not marry the shepherd!
His clothes are coarse; his wool is rough.
I will marry the farmer.
The farmer grows flax for my clothes.
The farmer grows barley for my table."

Dumuzi spoke:

"Why do you speak about the farmer?
Why do you speak about him?
If he gives you black flour,
I will give you black wool.
If he gives you white flour,
I will give you white wool.
If he gives you beer,
I will give you sweet milk.
If he gives you bread,
I will give you honey cheese.

I will give the farmer my leftover cream.
I will give the farmer my leftover milk.
Why do you speak about the farmer?
What does he have more than I do?"

Inanna spoke:

"Shepherd, without my mother, Ningal, you'd be driven away,
Without my grandmother, Ningikuga, you'd be driven into the
    steppes,
Without my father, Nanna, you'd have no roof,
Without my brother, Utu—"

Dumuzi spoke:

"Inanna, do not start a quarrel.
My father, Enki, is as good as your father, Nanna.
My mother, Sirtur, is as good as your mother, Ningal.
My sister, Geshtinanna, is as good as yours.
Queen of the palace, let us talk it over.

Inanna, let us sit and speak together.
I am as good as Utu.
Enki is as good as Nanna.
Sirtur is as good as Ningal.
Queen of the palace, let us talk it over."

The word they had spoken
Was a word of desire.
From the starting of the quarrel
Came the lovers' desire.

34

The shepherd went to the royal house with cream.
Dumuzi went to the royal house with milk.
Before the door, he called out:
> "Open the house, My Lady, open the house!"

Inanna ran to Ningal, the mother who bore her.
Ningal counseled her daughter, saying:
> "My child, the young man will be your father.
> My daughter, the young man will be your mother.
> He will treat you like a father.
> He will care for you like a mother.
> Open the house, My Lady, open the house!"

Inanna, at her mother's command,
Bathed and anointed herself with scented oil.
She covered her body with the royal white robe.
She readied her dowry.
She arranged her precious lapis beads around her neck.
She took her seal in her hand.

Dumuzi waited expectantly.

Inanna opened the door for him.
Inside the house she shone before him
Like the light of the moon.

Dumuzi looked at her joyously.
He pressed his neck close against hers.
He kissed her.

Inanna spoke:
    "What I tell you
      Let the singer weave into song.
      What I tell you,
      Let it flow from ear to mouth,
      Let it pass from old to young:

My vulva, the horn,
The Boat of Heaven,
Is full of eagerness like the young moon.
My untilled land lies fallow.

As for me, Inanna,
Who will plow my vulva?
Who will plow my high field?
Who will plow my wet ground?

As for me, the young woman,
Who will plow my vulva?
Who will station the ox there?
Who will plow my vulva?"

Dumuzi replied:
"Great Lady, the king will plow your vulva.
I, Dumuzi the King, will plow your vulva."

Inanna:
"Then plow my vulva, man of my heart!
Plow my vulva!"

At the king's lap stood the rising cedar.
Plants grew high by their side.
Grains grew high by their side.
Gardens flourished luxuriantly.

Inanna sang:

> "He has sprouted; he has burgeoned;
> He is lettuce planted by the water.
> He is the one my womb loves best.
>
> My well-stocked garden of the plain,
> My barley growing high in its furrow,
> My apple tree which bears fruit up to its crown,
> He is lettuce planted by the water.
>
> My honey-man, my honey-man sweetens me always.
> My lord, the honey-man of the gods,
> He is the one my womb loves best.
> His hand is honey, his foot is honey,
> He sweetens me always.
>
> My eager impetuous caresser of the navel,
> My caresser of the soft thighs,
> He is the one my womb loves best,
> He is lettuce planted by the water."

Dumuzi sang:

"O Lady, your breast is your field.
Inanna, your breast is your field.
Your broad field pours out plants.
Your broad field pours out grain.
Water flows from on high for your servant.
Bread flows from on high for your servant.
Pour it out for me, Inanna.
I will drink all you offer."

Inanna sang:

"Make your milk sweet and thick, my bridegroom.
My shepherd, I will drink your fresh milk.
Wild bull, Dumuzi, make your milk sweet and thick.
I will drink your fresh milk.

Let the milk of the goat flow in my sheepfold.
Fill my holy churn with honey cheese.
Lord Dumuzi, I will drink your fresh milk.

My husband, I will guard my sheepfold for you.
I will watch over your house of life, the storehouse,
The shining quivering place which delights Sumer—
The house which decides the fates of the land,
The house which gives the breath of life to the people.
I, the queen of the palace, will watch over your house."

Dumuzi spoke:

"My sister, I would go with you to my garden.

Inanna, I would go with you to my garden.

I would go with you to my orchard.

I would go with you to my apple tree.

There I would plant the sweet, honey-covered seed."

Inanna spoke:

"He brought me into his garden.

My brother, Dumuzi, brought me into his garden.

I strolled with him among the standing trees,

I stood with him among the fallen trees,

By an apple tree I knelt as is proper.

Before my brother coming in song,

Who rose to me out of the poplar leaves,

Who came to me in the midday heat,

Before my lord Dumuzi,

I poured out plants from my womb.

I placed plants before him,

I poured out plants before him.

I placed grain before him,

I poured out grain before him.

I poured out grain from my womb."

Inanna sang:

> "Last night as I, the queen, was shining bright,
> Last night as I, the Queen of Heaven, was shining bright,
> As I was shining bright and dancing,
> Singing praises at the coming of the night—
>
> He met me—he met me!
> My lord Dumuzi met me.
> He put his hand into my hand.
> He pressed his neck close against mine.
>
> My high priest is ready for the holy loins.
> My lord Dumuzi is ready for the holy loins.
> The plants and herbs in his field are ripe.
> O Dumuzi! Your fullness is my delight!"

She called for it, she called for it, she called for the bed!
She called for the bed that rejoices the heart.
She called for the bed that sweetens the loins.
She called for the bed of kingship.
She called for the bed of queenship.
Inanna called for the bed:

     "Let the bed that rejoices the heart be prepared!
      Let the bed that sweetens the loins be prepared!
      Let the bed of kingship be prepared!
      Let the bed of queenship be prepared!
      Let the royal bed be prepared!"

Inanna spread the bridal sheet across the bed.
She called to the king:

     "The bed is ready!"
She called to her bridegroom:

     "The bed is waiting!"

He put his hand in her hand.
He put his hand to her heart.
Sweet is the sleep of hand-to-hand.
Sweeter still the sleep of heart-to-heart.

Inanna spoke:

"I bathed for the wild bull,
I bathed for the shepherd Dumuzi,
I perfumed my sides with ointment,
I coated my mouth with sweet-smelling amber,
I painted my eyes with kohl.

He shaped my loins with his fair hands,
The shepherd Dumuzi filled my lap with cream and milk,
He stroked my pubic hair,
He watered my womb.
He laid his hands on my holy vulva,
He smoothed my black boat with cream,
He quickened my narrow boat with milk,
He caressed me on the bed.

Now I will caress my high priest on the bed,
I will caress the faithful shepherd Dumuzi,
I will caress his loins, the shepherdship of the land,
I will decree a sweet fate for him."

The Queen of Heaven,
The heroic woman, greater than her mother,
Who was presented the *me* by Enki,
Inanna, the First Daughter of the Moon,
Decreed the fate of Dumuzi:

"In battle I am your leader,
In combat I am your armor-bearer,
In the assembly I am your advocate,
On the campaign I am your inspiration.
You, the chosen shepherd of the holy shrine,
You, the king, the faithful provider of Uruk,
You, the light of An's great shrine,
In all ways you are fit:

To hold your head high on the lofty dais,
To sit on the lapis lazuli throne,
To cover your head with the holy crown,
To wear long clothes on your body,
To bind yourself with the garments of kingship,
To carry the mace and sword,
To guide straight the long bow and arrow,
To fasten the throw-stick and sling at your side,
To race on the road with the holy sceptre in your hand,
And the holy sandals on your feet,
To prance on the holy breast like a lapis lazuli calf.

You, the sprinter, the chosen shepherd,
In all ways you are fit.
May your heart enjoy long days.

That which An has determined for you—may it not be altered.
That which Enlil has granted—may it not be changed.
You are the favorite of Ningal.
Inanna holds you dear."

Ninshubur, the faithful servant of the holy shrine of Uruk,
Led Dumuzi to the sweet thighs of Inanna and spoke:
  "My queen, here is the choice of your heart,
    The king, your beloved bridegroom.
    May he spend long days in the sweetness of your holy loins.
    Give him a favorable and glorious reign.
    Grant him the king's throne, firm in its foundations.
    Grant him the shepherd's staff of judgment.
    Grant him the enduring crown with the radiant and noble
      diadem.

    From where the sun rises to where the sun sets,
    From south to north,
    From the Upper Sea to the Lower Sea,
    From the land of the *huluppu*-tree to the land of the cedar,
    Let his shepherd's staff protect all of Sumer and Akkad.

    As the farmer, let him make the fields fertile,
    As the shepherd, let him make the sheepfolds multiply,
    Under his reign let there be vegetation,
    Under his reign let there be rich grain.

    In the marshland may the fish and birds chatter,
    In the canebrake may the young and old reeds grow high,
    In the steppe may the *mashgur*-trees grow high,
    In the forests may the deer and wild goats multiply,
    In the orchards may there be honey and wine,

In the gardens may the lettuce and cress grow high,
In the palace may there be long life.
May there be floodwater in the Tigris and Euphrates,
May the plants grow high on their banks and fill the meadows,
May the Lady of Vegetation pile the grain in heaps and mounds.

O my Queen of Heaven and Earth,
Queen of all the universe,
 May he enjoy long days in the sweetness of your holy loins."

The king went with lifted head to the holy loins.
He went with lifted head to the loins of Inanna.
He went to the queen with lifted head.
He opened wide his arms to the holy priestess of heaven.

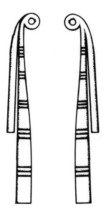

Inanna spoke:

> "My beloved, the delight of my eyes, met me.
> We rejoiced together.
> He took his pleasure of me.
> He brought me into his house.
>
> He laid me down on the fragrant honey-bed.
> My sweet love, lying by my heart,
> Tongue-playing, one by one,
> My fair Dumuzi did so fifty times.
>
> Now, my sweet love is sated.
> Now he says:
> 'Set me free, my sister, set me free.
> You will be a little daughter to my father.
> Come, my beloved sister, I would go to the palace.
> Set me free . . .' "

Inanna spoke:

"My blossom-bearer, your allure was sweet.
My blossom-bearer in the apple orchard,
My bearer of fruit in the apple orchard,
Dumuzi-*abzu*, your allure was sweet.

My fearless one,
My holy statue,
My statue outfitted with sword and lapis lazuli diadem,
How sweet was your allure. . . ."

THE DESCENT OF INANNA

FROM THE GREAT ABOVE
TO THE GREAT BELOW

From the Great Above she opened her ear to the Great Below.
From the Great Above the goddess opened her ear to the Great Below.
From the Great Above Inanna opened her ear to the Great Below.

My Lady abandoned heaven and earth to descend to the underworld.
Inanna abandoned heaven and earth to descend to the underworld.
She abandoned her office of holy priestess to descend to the underworld.

In Uruk she abandoned her temple to descend to the underworld.
In Badtibira she abandoned her temple to descend to the underworld.
In Zabalam she abandoned her temple to descend to the underworld.
In Adab she abandoned her temple to descend to the underworld.
In Nippur she abandoned her temple to descend to the underworld.
In Kish she abandoned her temple to descend to the underworld.
In Akkad she abandoned her temple to descend to the underworld.

She gathered together the seven *me*.
She took them into her hands.
With the *me* in her possession, she prepared herself:

She placed the *shugurra*, the crown of the steppe, on her head.
She arranged the dark locks of hair across her forehead.
She tied the small lapis beads around her neck,
Let the double strand of beads fall to her breast,
And wrapped the royal robe around her body.
She daubed her eyes with ointment called "Let him come,
   Let him come,"
Bound the breastplate called "Come, man, come!" around her chest,
Slipped the gold ring over her wrist,
And took the lapis measuring rod and line in her hand.

Inanna set out for the underworld.
Ninshubur, her faithful servant, went with her.
Inanna spoke to her, saying:
   "Ninshubur, my constant support,
      My *sukkal* who gives me wise advice,
      My warrior who fights by my side,
      I am descending to the *kur,* to the underworld.
      If I do not return,
      Set up a lament for me by the ruins.
      Beat the drum for me in the assembly places.
      Circle the houses of the gods.
      Tear at your eyes, at your mouth, at your thighs.
      Dress yourself in a single garment like a beggar.
      Go to Nippur, to the temple of Enlil.

When you enter his holy shrine, cry out:
'O Father Enlil, do not let your daughter
Be put to death in the underworld.
Do not let your bright silver
Be covered with the dust of the underworld.
Do not let your precious lapis
Be broken into stone for the stoneworker.
Do not let your fragrant boxwood
Be cut into wood for the woodworker.
Do not let the holy priestess of heaven
Be put to death in the underworld.'

If Enlil will not help you,
Go to Ur, to the temple of Nanna.
Weep before Father Nanna.
If Nanna will not help you,
Go to Eridu, to the temple of Enki.
Weep before Father Enki.
Father Enki, the God of Wisdom, knows the food of life,
He knows the water of life;
He knows the secrets.
Surely he will not let me die."

Inanna continued on her way to the underworld.
Then she stopped and said:
    "Go now, Ninshubur—
    Do not forget the words I have commanded you."

When Inanna arrived at the outer gates of the underworld,
She knocked loudly.

She cried out in a fierce voice:

> "Open the door, gatekeeper!
> Open the door, Neti!
> I alone would enter!"

Neti, the chief gatekeeper of the *kur,* asked:

> "Who are you?"

She answered:

> "I am Inanna, Queen of Heaven,
> On my way to the East."

Neti said:

> "If you are truly Inanna, Queen of Heaven,
> On your way to the East,
> Why has your heart led you on the road
> From which no traveler returns?"

Inanna answered:

puts Ereshkigal in older generations of gods

> "Because . . . of my older sister, Ereshkigal,
> Her husband, Gugalanna, the Bull of Heaven, has died.
> I have come to witness the funeral rites.
> Let the beer of his funeral rites be poured into the cup.
> Let it be done."

Here, Inanna is controlling -- or trying to -- the happenings of the underworld

Neti spoke:

> "Stay here, Inanna, I will speak to my queen.
> I will give her your message."

Neti, the chief gatekeeper of the *kur,*
Entered the palace of Ereshkigal, the Queen of the Underworld,
 and said:
 "My queen, a maid
   As tall as heaven,
   As wide as the earth,
   As strong as the foundations of the city wall,
   Waits outside the palace gates.

   She has gathered together the seven *me.*
   She has taken them into her hands.
   With the *me* in her possession, she has prepared herself:

   On her head she wears the *shugurra,* the crown of the steppe.
   Across her forehead her dark locks of hair are carefully
     arranged.
   Around her neck she wears the small lapis beads.
   At her breast she wears the double strand of beads.
   Her body is wrapped with the royal robe.
   Her eyes are daubed with the ointment called, 'Let him come,
     let him come.'
   Around her chest she wears the breastplate called 'Come, man,
     come!'
   On her wrist she wears the gold ring.
   In her hand she carries the lapis measuring rod and line."

When Ereshkigal heard this,
She slapped her thigh and bit her lip.
She took the matter into her heart and dwelt on it.
Then she spoke:

"Come, Neti, my chief gatekeeper of the *kur*,
Heed my words:
Bolt the seven gates of the underworld.
Then, one by one, open each gate a crack.
Let Inanna enter.
As she enters, remove her royal garments.
Let the holy priestess of heaven enter bowed low."

Neti heeded the words of his queen.
He bolted the seven gates of the underworld.
Then he opened the outer gate.
He said to the maid:
        "Come, Inanna, enter."

When she entered the first gate,
From her head, the *shugurra*, the crown of the steppe, was removed.

Inanna asked:
        "What is this?"

She was told:

> "Quiet, Inanna, the ways of the underworld are perfect.
> They may not be questioned."

When she entered the second gate,
From her neck the small lapis beads were removed.

Inanna asked:

> "What is this?"

She was told:

> "Quiet, Inanna, the ways of the underworld are perfect.
> They may not be questioned."

When she entered the third gate,
From her breast the double strand of beads was removed.

Inanna asked:

> "What is this?"

She was told:

> "Quiet, Inanna, the ways of the underworld are perfect.
> They may not be questioned."

When she entered the fourth gate,
From her chest the breastplate called "Come, man, come!"
    was removed.

Inanna asked:

> "What is this?"

She was told:
> "Quiet, Inanna, the ways of the underworld are perfect.
> They may not be questioned."

When she entered the fifth gate,
From her wrist the gold ring was removed.

Inanna asked:
> "What is this?"

She was told:
> "Quiet, Inanna, the ways of the underworld are perfect.
> They may not be questioned."

When she entered the sixth gate,
From her hand the lapis measuring rod and line was removed.

Inanna asked:
> "What is this?"

She was told:
> "Quiet, Inanna, the ways of the underworld are perfect.
> They may not be questioned."

When she entered the seventh gate,
From her body the royal robe was removed.

Inanna asked:
> "What is this?"

She was told:

> "Quiet, Inanna, the ways of the underworld are perfect.
> They may not be questioned."

Naked and bowed low, Inanna entered the throne room.
Ereshkigal rose from her throne.
Inanna started toward the throne.
The Annuna, the judges of the underworld, surrounded her.
They passed judgment against her.

Then Ereshkigal fastened on Inanna the eye of death.
She spoke against her the word of wrath.
She uttered against her the cry of guilt.

She struck her.

Inanna was turned into a corpse,
A piece of rotting meat,
And was hung from a hook on the wall.

When, after three days and three nights, Inanna had not returned,
Ninshubur set up a lament for her by the ruins.
She beat the drum for her in the assembly places.
She circled the houses of the gods.
She tore at her eyes; she tore at her mouth; she tore at her thighs.
She dressed herself in a single garment like a beggar.
Alone, she set out for Nippur and the temple of Enlil.

When she entered the holy shrine,
She cried out:

"O Father Enlil, do not let your daughter
Be put to death in the underworld.
Do not let your bright silver
Be covered with the dust of the underworld.
Do not let your precious lapis
Be broken into stone for the stoneworker.
Do not let your fragrant boxwood
Be cut into wood for the woodworker.
Do not let the holy priestess of heaven
Be put to death in the underworld."

Father Enlil answered angrily:
"My daughter craved the Great Above.
Inanna craved the Great Below.
She who receives the *me* of the underworld does not return.
She who goes to the Dark City stays there."

Father Enlil would not help.

61

Ninshubur went to Ur and the temple of Nanna.
When she entered the holy shrine,
She cried out:

>"O Father Nanna, do not let your daughter
>Be put to death in the underworld.
>Do not let your bright silver
>Be covered with the dust of the underworld.
>Do not let your precious lapis
>Be broken into stone for the stoneworker.
>Do not let your fragrant boxwood
>Be cut into wood for the woodworker.
>Do not let the holy priestess of heaven.
>Be put to death in the underworld."

Father Nanna answered angrily:

>"My daughter craved the Great Above.
>Inanna craved the Great Below.
>She who receives the *me* of the underworld does not return.
>She who goes to the Dark City stays there.

Father Nanna would not help.

Ninshubur went to Eridu and the temple of Enki.
When she entered the holy shrine,
She cried out:

>"O Father Enki, do not let your daughter
>Be put to death in the underworld.
>Do not let your bright silver
>Be covered with the dust of the underworld.

Do not let your precious lapis
Be broken into stone for the stoneworker.
Do not let your fragrant boxwood
Be cut into wood for the woodworker.
Do not let the holy priestess of heaven
Be put to death in the underworld."

Father Enki said:
    "What has happened?
    What has my daughter done?
    Inanna! Queen of All the Lands! Holy Priestess of Heaven!
    What has happened?
    I am troubled. I am grieved."

From under his fingernail Father Enki brought forth dirt.

He fashioned the dirt into a *kurgarra,* a creature neither male nor female.

From under the fingernail of his other hand he brought forth dirt.

He fashioned the dirt into a *galatur,* a creature neither male nor female.

He gave the food of life to the *kurgarra.*

He gave the water of life to the *galatur.*

Enki spoke to the *kurgarra* and *galatur,* saying:

>"Go to the underworld,
>
>>Enter the door like flies.
>>
>>Ereshkigal, the Queen of the Underworld, is moaning
>>
>>With the cries of a woman about to give birth.
>>
>>No linen is spread over her body.
>>
>>Her breasts are uncovered.
>>
>>Her hair swirls about her head like leeks.
>>
>>When she cries, 'Oh! Oh! My inside!'
>>
>>Cry also, 'Oh! Oh! Your inside!'
>>
>>When she cries, 'Oh! Oh! My outside!'
>>
>>Cry also, 'Oh! Oh! Your outside!'
>>
>>The queen will be pleased.
>>
>>She will offer you a gift.
>>
>>Ask her only for the corpse that hangs from the hook on the wall.
>>
>>One of you will sprinkle the food of life on it.
>>
>>The other will sprinkle the water of life.
>>
>>Inanna will arise."

The *kurgarra* and the *galatur* heeded Enki's words.

They set out for the underworld.

Like flies, they slipped through the cracks of the gates.

They entered the throne room of the Queen of the Underworld.

No linen was spread over her body.
Her breasts were uncovered.
Her hair swirled around her head like leeks.

Ereshkigal was moaning:
"Oh! Oh! My inside!"

They moaned:
"Oh! Oh! Your inside!"

She moaned:
"Ohhhh! Oh! My outside!"

They moaned:
"Ohhhh! Oh! Your outside!"

She groaned:
"Oh! Oh! My belly!"

They groaned:
"Oh! Oh! Your belly!"

She groaned:
"Oh! Ohhhh! My back!!"

They groaned:
"Oh! Ohhhh! Your back!!"

She sighed:

    "Ah! Ah! My heart!"

They sighed:

    "Ah! Ah! Your heart!"

She sighed:

    "Ah! Ahhhh! My liver!"

They sighed:

    "Ah! Ahhhh! Your liver!"

Ereshkigal stopped.
She looked at them.
She asked:

    "Who are you,
      Moaning—groaning—sighing with me?
      If you are gods, I will bless you.
      If you are mortals, I will give you a gift.
      I will give you the water-gift, the river in its fullness."

The *kurgarra* and *galatur* answered:

    "We do not wish it."

Ereshkigal said:

    "I will give you the grain-gift, the fields in harvest."

The *kurgarra* and *galatur* said:

    "We do not wish it."

Ereshkigal said:

"Speak then! What do you wish?"

They answered:

"We wish only the corpse that hangs from the hook on the
wall."

Ereshkigal said:

"The corpse belongs to Inanna."

They said:

"Whether it belongs to our queen,
Whether it belongs to our king,
That is what we wish."

The corpse was given to them.

The *kurgarra* sprinkled the food of life on the corpse.
The *galatur* sprinkled the water of life on the corpse.
Inanna arose. . . .

Inanna was about to ascend from the underworld
When the Annuna, the judges of the underworld, seized her.
They said:

>"No one ascends from the underworld unmarked.
>If Inanna wishes to return from the underworld,
>She must provide someone in her place."

As Inanna ascended from the underworld,
The *galla,* the demons of the underworld, clung to her side.
The *galla* were demons who know no food, who know no drink,
Who eat no offerings, who drink no libations,
Who accept no gifts.
They enjoy no lovemaking.
They have no sweet children to kiss.
They tear the wife from the husband's arms,
They tear the child from the father's knees,
They steal the bride from her marriage home.

The demons clung to Inanna.
The small *galla* who accompanied Inanna
Were like reeds the size of low picket fences.
The large *galla* who accompanied Inanna
Were like reeds the size of high picket fences.

The one who walked in front of Inanna was not a minister,
Yet he carried a sceptre.
The one who walked behind her was not a warrior,
Yet he carried a mace.
Ninshubur, dressed in a soiled sackcloth,

Waited outside the palace gates.
When she saw Inanna
Surrounded by the *galla,*
She threw herself in the dust at Inanna's feet.

The *galla* said:
> "Walk on, Inanna,
> We will take Ninshubur in your place."

Inanna cried:
> "No! Ninshubur is my constant support.
> She is my *sukkal* who gives me wise advice.
> She is my warrior who fights by my side.
> She did not forget my words.
>
> She set up a lament for me by the ruins.
> She beat the drum for me at the assembly places.
> She circled the houses of the gods.
> She tore at her eyes, at her mouth, at her thighs.
> She dressed herself in a single garment like a beggar.
>
> Alone, she set out for Nippur and the temple of Enlil.
> She went to Ur and the temple of Nanna.
> She went to Eridu and the temple of Enki.
> Because of her, my life was saved.
> I will never give Ninshubur to you."

The *galla* said:
> "Walk on, Inanna,
> We will accompany you to Umma."

In Umma, at the holy shrine,

Shara, the son of Inanna, was dressed in a soiled sackcloth.

When he saw Inanna

Surrounded by the *galla,*

He threw himself in the dust at her feet.

The *galla* said:

    "Walk on to your city, Inanna,

      We will take Shara in your place."

Inanna cried:

    "No! Not Shara!

    He is my son who sings hymns to me.

    He is my son who cuts my nails and smooths my hair.

    I will never give Shara to you."

The *galla* said:

    "Walk on, Inanna,

      We will accompany you to Badtibira."

In Badtibira, at the holy shrine,

Lulal, the son of Inanna, was dressed in a soiled sackcloth.

When he saw Inanna

Surrounded by the *galla,*

He threw himself in the dust at her feet.

The *galla* said:

    "Walk on to your city, Inanna,

      We will take Lulal in your place."

Inanna cried:

"Not Lulal! He is my son.

He is a leader among men.

He is my right arm. He is my left arm.

I will never give Lulal to you."

The *galla* said:

"Walk on to your city, Inanna.

We will go with you to the big apple tree in Uruk."

In Uruk, by the big apple tree,
Dumuzi, the husband of Inanna, was dressed in his shining *me-* garments.
He sat on his magnificent throne; (he did not move).

The *galla* seized him by his thighs.
They poured milk out of his seven churns.
They broke the reed pipe which the shepherd was playing.

Inanna fastened on Dumuzi the eye of death.
She spoke against him the word of wrath.
She uttered against him the cry of guilt:

"Take him! Take Dumuzi away!"

The *galla,* who know no food, who know no drink,
Who eat no offerings, who drink no libations,
Who accept no gifts, seized Dumuzi.
They made him stand up; they made him sit down.
They beat the husband of Inanna.
They gashed him with axes.

Dumuzi let out a wail.
He raised his hands to heaven to Utu, the God of Justice,
  and beseeched him:

> "O Utu, you are my brother-in-law,
>   I am the husband of your sister.
>   I brought cream to your mother's house,
>   I brought milk to Ningal's house.
>   I am the one who carried food to the holy shrine.
>   I am the one who brought wedding gifts to Uruk.
>   I am the one who danced on the holy knees, the knees of
>   Inanna.
>
>   Utu, you who are a just god, a merciful god,
>   Change my hands into the hands of a snake.
>   Change my feet into the feet of a snake.
>   Let me escape from my demons;
>   Do not let them hold me."

The merciful Utu accepted Dumuzi's tears.
He changed the hands of Dumuzi into snake hands.
He changed the feet of Dumuzi into snake feet.
Dumuzi escaped from his demons.
They could not hold him. . . .

THE DREAM OF DUMUZI

His heart was filled with tears.
The shepherd's heart was filled with tears.
Dumuzi's heart was filled with tears.
Dumuzi stumbled across the steppe, weeping:
    "O steppe, set up a wail for me!
    O crabs in the river, mourn for me!
    O frogs in the river, call for me!
    O my mother, Sirtur, weep for me!

    If she does not find the five breads,
    If she does not find the ten breads,
    If she does not know the day I am dead,
    You, O steppe, tell her, tell my mother.
    On the steppe, my mother will shed tears for me.
    On the steppe, my little sister will mourn for me."

He lay down to rest.
The shepherd lay down to rest.
Dumuzi lay down to rest.

As he lay among the buds and rushes,
He dreamed a dream.
He awoke from his dream.
He trembled from his vision.
He rubbed his eyes, terrified.

Dumuzi called out:
"Bring . . . bring her . . . bring my sister.
Bring my Geshtinanna, my little sister,
My tablet-knowing scribe, ← means she can read
My singer who knows many songs,
My sister who knows the meaning of words,
My wise woman who knows the meaning of dreams.
I must speak to her.
I must tell her my dream."

Dumuzi spoke to Geshtinanna, saying:
"A dream! My sister, listen to my dream:
Rushes rise all about me; rushes grow thick about me.
A single growing reed trembles for me.
From a double-growing reed, first one, then the other,
    is removed.
In a wooded grove, the terror of tall trees rises about me.
Water is poured over my holy hearth.
The bottom of my churn drops away.
My drinking cup falls from its peg.
My shepherd's crook has disappeared.

75

An eagle seizes a lamb from the sheepfold.
A falcon catches a sparrow on the reed fence.

My sister, your goats drag their lapis beards in the dust.
Your sheep scratch the earth with bent feet.

The churn lies silent; no milk is poured.
The cup lies shattered; Dumuzi is no more.
The sheepfold is given to the winds."

Geshtinanna spoke:

"My brother, do not tell me your dream.
Dumuzi, do not tell me such a dream.

The rushes which rise all about you,
The rushes which grow thick about you,
Are your demons, who will pursue and attack you.

The single growing reed which trembles for you
Is our mother; she will mourn for you.

The double-growing reed, from which one, then the other, is
    removed, Dumuzi,
Is you and I; first one, then the other, will be taken away.

In the wooded grove, the terror of tall trees which rises about
    you
Is the *galla*; they will descend on you in the sheepfold.

When the fire is put out on your holy hearth,
The sheepfold will become a house of desolation.

When the bottom of your churn drops away,
You will be held by the *galla*.

When your drinking cup falls from its peg,

You will fall to the earth, onto your mother's knees.

When your shepherd's crook disappears,
The *galla* will cause everything to wither.

The eagle who seizes a lamb in the sheepfold
Is the *galla* who will scratch your cheeks.

The falcon who catches a sparrow in the reed fence
Is the *galla* who will climb the fence to take you away.

Dumuzi, my goats drag their lapis beards in the dust.

My hair will swirl around in heaven for you.
My sheep scratch the earth with bent feet.
O Dumuzi, I will tear at my cheeks in grief for you.

The churn lies silent; no milk is poured.
The cup lies shattered; Dumuzi is no more.
The sheepfold is given to the winds—"

Scarcely had she spoken these words
When Dumuzi cried out:
      "My sister! Quickly, go up the hill!
      Do not go with slow noble steps.
      Sister, run!
      The *galla,* hated and feared by men,
      Are coming on the boats.
      They carry wood to bind the hands;
      They carry wood to bind the neck.
      Sister, run!"

Geshtinanna went up the hill.
Dumuzi's friend went with her.

Dumuzi cried:

> "Do you see them?"

The friend cried:

> "They are coming;
> The large *galla* who carry wood to bind the neck,
> They are coming for you."

Geshtinanna cried:

> "Quickly, brother!
> Hide your head in the grass.
> Your demons are coming for you."

Dumuzi said:

> "My sister, tell no one my hiding place.
> My friend, tell no one my hiding place.
> I will hide in the grass.
> I will hide among the small plants.
> I will hide among the large plants.
> I will hide in the ditches of Arali."

Geshtinanna and Dumuzi's friend answered:

> "Dumuzi, if we tell your hiding place,
> Let your dogs devour us,
> Your black dogs of shepherdship,
> Your royal dogs of kingship,
> Let your dogs devour us!"

The small *galla* spoke to the large *galla:*

> "You *galla,* who have no mother, or father,
> No sister, brother, wife, or child,

You who flutter over heaven and earth like wardens,
Who cling to a man's side,
Who show no favor,
Who know not good from evil,
Tell us,
Who has ever seen the soul of a frightened man
Living in peace?
Let us not look for Dumuzi in the home of his friend.
Let us not look for Dumuzi in the home of his brother-in-law.
Let us look for Dumuzi in the home of his sister, Geshtinanna."

The *galla* clapped their hands gleefully.
They went searching for Dumuzi.
They came to the home of Geshtinanna. They cried out:
    "Show us where your brother is!"

Geshtinanna would not speak.

They offered her the water-gift.
She refused it.
They offered her the grain-gift.
She refused it.

Heaven was brought close.
Earth was brought close.
Geshtinanna would not speak.

They tore her clothes.
They poured pitch into her vulva.
Geshtinanna would not speak.

The small *galla* said to the large *galla:*
>"Who since the beginning of time
>> Has ever known a sister to reveal a brother's hiding place?
>> Come, let us look for Dumuzi in the home of his friend."

The *galla* went to Dumuzi's friend.
They offered him the water-gift.
He accepted it.
They offered him the grain-gift.
He accepted it.
He said:
>"Dumuzi hid in the grass,
>> But I do not know the place."

The *galla* searched for Dumuzi in the grass.
They did not find him.
The friend said:
>"Dumuzi hid among the small plants,
>> But I do not know the place."

The *galla* searched for Dumuzi among the small plants.
They did not find him.
The friend said:
>"Dumuzi hid among the large plants,
>> But I do not know the place."

The *galla* searched for Dumuzi among the large plants.
They did not find him.
The friend said:
>"Dumuzi hid in the ditches of Arali.
>> Dumuzi fell down in the ditches of Arali."

In the ditches of Arali, the *galla* caught Dumuzi.
Dumuzi turned pale and wept.
He cried out:

> "My sister saved my life.
>> My friend caused my death.
>> If my sister's child wanders in the street,
>> Let the child be protected—let the child be blessed.
>> If my friend's child wanders in the street,
>> Let the child be lost—let the child be cursed."

The *galla* surrounded Dumuzi.
They bound his hands; they bound his neck.
They beat the husband of Inanna.
Dumuzi raised his arms to heaven, to Utu, the God of Justice,
  and cried out:

> "O Utu, you are my brother-in-law,
>> I am the husband of your sister.
>> I am the one who carried food to the holy shrine.
>> I am the one who brought wedding gifts to Uruk.
>> I kissed the holy lips,
>> I danced on the holy knees, the knees of Inanna.
>>
>> Change my hands into the hands of a gazelle.
>> Change my feet into the feet of a gazelle.
>> Let me escape from my demons.
>> Let me flee to Kubiresh!"

The merciful Utu accepted Dumuzi's tears.
He changed his hands into the hands of a gazelle.
He changed his feet into the feet of a gazelle.
Dumuzi escaped from his demons.
He fled to Kubiresh.

The *galla* said:
"Let us go to Kubiresh!"

The *galla* arrived in Kubiresh.
Dumuzi escaped from his demons.
He fled to Old Belili.

The *galla* said:
"Let us go to Old Belili!"

Dumuzi entered the house of Old Belili. He said to her:
"Old woman. I am not a mere mortal.
I am the husband of the goddess Inanna.
Pour water for me to drink.
Sprinkle flour for me to eat."

After the old woman poured water
And sprinkled flour for Dumuzi,
She left the house.

When the *galla* saw her leave, they entered the house.
Dumuzi escaped from his demons.
He fled to the sheepfold of his sister, Geshtinanna.

When Geshtinanna found Dumuzi in the sheepfold, she wept.
She brought her mouth close to heaven.
She brought her mouth close to earth.
Her grief covered the horizon like a garment.

She tore at her eyes.
She tore at her mouth.
She tore at her thighs.

The *galla* climbed the reed fence.
The first *galla* struck Dumuzi on the cheek with a piercing nail,
The second *galla* struck Dumuzi on the other cheek with the shepherd's
    crook,
The third *galla* smashed the bottom of the churn,
The fourth *galla* threw the drinking cup down from its peg,
The fifth *galla* shattered the churn,
The sixth *galla* shattered the cup,
The seventh *galla* cried:

> "Rise, Dumuzi!
> Husband of Inanna, son of Sirtur, brother of Geshtinanna!
> Rise from your false sleep!
> Your ewes are seized! Your lambs are seized!
> Your goats are seized! Your kids are seized!

Take off your holy crown from your head!
Take off your *me-* garment from your body!
Let your royal sceptre fall to the ground!
Take off your holy sandals from your feet!
Naked, you go with us!"

The *galla* seized Dumuzi.
They surrounded him.
They bound his hands. They bound his neck.

The churn was silent. No milk was poured.
The cup was shattered. Dumuzi was no more.
The sheepfold was given to the winds.

THE RETURN

A lament was raised in the city:

> "My Lady weeps bitterly for her young husband.
> Inanna weeps bitterly for her young husband.
> Woe for her husband! Woe for her young love!
> Woe for her house! Woe for her city!
>
> Dumuzi was taken captive in Uruk.
> He will no longer bathe in Eridu.
> He will no longer soap himself at the holy shrine.
> He will no longer treat the mother of Inanna as his mother.
> He will no longer perform his sweet task
> Among the maidens of the city.
>
> He will no longer compete with the young men of the city.
> He will no longer raise his sword higher than the *kurgarra*
>   priests.
> Great is the grief of those who mourn for Dumuzi."

Inanna wept for Dumuzi:

> "Gone is my husband, my sweet husband.
> Gone is my love, my sweet love.
> My beloved has been taken from the city.
> O, you flies of the steppe,
> My beloved bridegroom has been taken from me
> Before I could wrap him with a proper shroud.
>
> The wild bull lives no more.
> The shepherd, the wild bull lives no more.
> Dumuzi, the wild bull, lives no more.
>
> I ask the hills and valleys:
> 'Where is my husband?'
> I say to them:
> 'I can no longer bring him food.
> I can no longer serve him drink.'
>
> The jackal lies down in his bed.
> The raven dwells in his sheepfold.
> You ask me about his reed pipe?
> The wind must play it for him.
> You ask me about his sweet songs?
> The wind must sing them for him."

Sirtur, the mother of Dumuzi, wept for her son:

> "My heart plays the reed pipe of mourning.
> Once my boy wandered so freely on the steppe,
> Now he is captive.
> Once Dumuzi wandered so freely on the steppe,
> Now he is bound.

The ewe gives up her lamb.
The goat gives up her kid.
My heart plays the reed pipe of mourning.

O treacherous steppe!
In the place where he once said
'My mother will ask for me,'
Now he cannot move his hands.
He cannot move his feet.

My heart plays the reed pipe of mourning.
I would go to him,
I would see my child."

The mother walked to the desolate place.
Sirtur walked to where Dumuzi lay.
She looked at the slain wild bull.
She looked into his face. She said:
     "My child, the face is yours.
     The spirit has fled."

There is mourning in the house.
There is grief in the inner chambers.

The sister wandered about the city, weeping for her brother.
Geshtinanna wandered about the city, weeping for Dumuzi:
     "O my brother! Who is your sister?
     I am your sister.
     O Dumuzi! Who is your mother?
     I am your mother.

The day that dawns for you will also dawn for me.
The day that you will see I will also see.

I would find my brother! I would comfort him!
I would share his fate!"

When she saw the sister's grief,
When Inanna saw the grief of Geshtinanna,
She spoke to her gently:
> "Your brother's house is no more.
> Dumuzi has been carried away by the *galla*.
> I would take you to him,
> But I do not know the place."

Then a fly appeared.
The holy fly circled the air above Inanna's head and spoke:
> "If I tell you where Dumuzi is,
> What will you give me?"

Inanna said:
> "If you tell me,
> I will let you frequent the beer-houses and taverns.
> I will let you dwell among the talk of the wise ones.
> I will let you dwell among the songs of the minstrels."

The fly spoke:
> "Lift your eyes to the edges of the steppe,
> Lift your eyes to Arali.

There you will find Geshtinanna's brother,
There you will find the shepherd Dumuzi."

Inanna and Geshtinanna went to the edges of the steppe.
They found Dumuzi weeping.
Inanna took Dumuzi by the hand and said:
"You will go to the underworld
Half the year.
Your sister, since she has asked,
Will go the other half.
On the day you are called,
That day you will be taken.
On the day Geshtinanna is called,
That day you will be set free."

Inanna placed Dumuzi in the hands of the eternal.

Holy Ereshkigal! Great is your renown!
Holy Ereshkigal! I sing your praises!

SEVEN HYMNS
TO INANNA

THE HOLY PRIESTESS OF HEAVEN

I say, "Hail!" to the Holy One who appears in the heavens!
I say, "Hail!" to the Holy Priestess of Heaven!
I say, "Hail!" to Inanna, Great Lady of Heaven!

Holy Torch! You fill the sky with light!
You brighten the day at dawn!

I say, "Hail!" to Inanna, Great Lady of Heaven!

Awesome Lady of the Annuna Gods! Crowned with great horns,
You fill the heavens and earth with light!

I say, "Hail!" to Inanna, First Daughter of the Moon!

Mighty, majestic, and radiant,
You shine brilliantly in the evening,
You brighten the day at dawn,
You stand in the heavens like the sun and the moon,
Your wonders are known both above and below,
To the greatness of the holy priestess of heaven,
To you, Inanna, I sing!

LOUD THUNDERING STORM

Proud Queen of the Earth Gods, Supreme Among the Heaven Gods,
Loud Thundering Storm, you pour your rain over all the lands and all
    the people.
You make the heavens tremble and the earth quake.
Great Priestess, who can soothe your troubled heart?

You flash like lightning over the highlands; you throw your firebrands
    across the earth.
Your deafening command, whistling like the South Wind, splits apart
    great mountains.
You trample the disobedient like a wild bull; heaven and earth tremble.
Holy Priestess, who can soothe your troubled heart?

Your frightful cry descending from the heavens devours its victims.
Your quivering hand causes the midday heat to hover over the sea.
Your nighttime stalking of the heavens chills the land with its dark
    breeze.
Holy Inanna, the riverbanks overflow with the flood-waves of your
    heart. . . .

On the seventh day when the crescent moon reaches its fullness,
You bathe and sprinkle your face with holy water.
You cover your body with the long woolen garments of queenship.
You fasten combat and battle to your side;
You tie them into a girdle and let them rest.

In Eridu you received the *me* from the God of Wisdom,
Father Enki presented the *me* to you at his holy shrine in Eridu.
He placed queenship and godship in your hands.

You mount the steps to your high throne.
In all majesty you sit there
With your beloved husband, Dumuzi, at your side.

The gods of the land, wishing to hear their fate, come before you.
The gods of heaven and earth kneel before you.
The living creatures and the people of Sumer come before you.
The people of Sumer who parade before you
Are caught in your gaze,
And held in your holy yoke.

96

THE HOLY ONE

The people of Sumer parade before you.
They play the sweet *ala-*drums before you.
The people of Sumer parade before you.

I say, "Hail!" to Inanna, Great Lady of Heaven!

They beat the holy drum and timpani before you.
The people of Sumer parade before you.

I say, "Hail!" to Inanna, Great Lady of Heaven!

They play the holy harp and timpani before you.
The people of Sumer parade before you.

I say, "Hail!" to Inanna, First Daughter of the Moon!

The male prostitutes comb their hair before you.
They decorate the napes of their necks with colored scarfs,
They drape the cloak of the gods about their shoulders.
The righteous man and woman walk before you.
They hold the soothing harp by their sides.
Those who follow wear the sword belt.
They grasp the spear in their hands.

The people of Sumer parade before you.

The women adorn their right side with men's clothing.
The people of Sumer parade before you.

I say, "Hail!" to Inanna, Great Lady of Heaven!

The men adorn their left side with women's clothing.
The people of Sumer parade before you.

I say, "Hail!" to Inanna, Great Lady of Heaven!

The people compete with jump ropes and colored cords
The people of Sumer parade before you.

I say, "Hail!" to Inanna, First Daughter of the Moon!

The young men, who carry hoops, sing to you.
The maidens and coiffured priestesses walk before you,
They carry the sword and double-edged ax.
The ascending *kurgarra* priests raise their swords before you.
The priest, who covers his sword with blood, sprinkles blood,
He sprinkles blood over the throne of the court chamber.
The *tigi-* drum, the *sem-* drum, and the *ala-* tambourine resound!

In the heavens the Holy One appears alone.

My Lady looks in sweet wonder from heaven.
She looks in sweet wonder on all the lands
And on the people of Sumer as numerous as sheep.

THE LADY OF THE EVENING

At the end of the day, the Radiant Star, the Great Light that fills the
  sky,
The Lady of the Evening appears in the heavens.
The people in all the lands lift their eyes to her.
The men purify themselves; the women cleanse themselves.
The ox in his yoke lows to her.
The sheep stir up the dust in their fold.
All the living creatures of the steppe,
The four-footed creatures of the high steppe,
The lush gardens and orchards, the green reeds and trees,
The fish of the deep and the birds in the heavens—
My Lady makes them all hurry to their sleeping places.

The living creatures and the numerous people of Sumer kneel before
  her.
Those chosen by the old women prepare great platters of food and
  drink for her.
The Lady refreshes herself in the land.
There is great joy in Sumer.
The young man makes love with his beloved.

My Lady looks in sweet wonder from heaven.
The people of Sumer parade before the holy Inanna.
Inanna, the Lady of the Evening, is radiant.
I sing your praises, holy Inanna.
The Lady of the Evening is radiant on the horizon.

THE LADY OF THE MORNING

Honored Counselor, Ornament of Heaven, Joy of An!
When sweet sleep has ended in the bedchamber,
You appear like bright daylight.

When all the lands and the people of Sumer assemble,
Those sleeping on the roofs and those sleeping by the walls,
When they sing your praises, bringing their concerns to you,
You study their words.

You render a cruel judgment against the evildoer;
You destroy the wicked.
You look with kindly eyes on the straightforward;
You give that one your blessing.

My Lady looks in sweet wonder from heaven.
The people of Sumer parade before the holy Inanna.
Inanna, the Lady of the Morning, is radiant.
I sing your praises, holy Inanna.
The Lady of the Morning is radiant on the horizon.

THE LADY WHO ASCENDS
INTO THE HEAVENS

My Lady, the Amazement of the Land, the Lone Star,
The Brave One who appears first in the heavens—
All the lands fear her.

In the pure places of the steppe,
On the high roofs of the dwellings,
On the platforms of the city,
They make offerings to her:
Piles of incense like sweet-smelling cedar,
Fine sheep, fat sheep, long-haired sheep, *bull*
Butter, cheese, dates, fruits of all kinds.

They purify the earth for My Lady.
They celebrate her in song.
They fill the table of the land with the first fruits. *1st fruits of the harvest*
They pour dark beer for her.
They pour light beer for her.
Dark beer, emmer beer, *kind of wheat*
Emmer beer for My Lady.

The *sagub*-vat and the *lamsari*-vat make a bubbling noise for her. *cooking*

They prepare *gug*-bread in date syrup for her.

Flour, flour in honey, beer at dawn.

They pour wine and honey for her at sunrise.

cooking
something
for
Inanna

The gods and the people of Sumer go to her with food and drink.

They feed Inanna in the pure clean place.

My Lady looks in sweet wonder from heaven.

The people of Sumer parade before the holy Inanna.

Inanna, the Lady Who Ascends into the Heavens, is radiant.

I sing your praises, holy Inanna.

The Lady Who Ascends into the Heavens is radiant on the horizon.

THE JOY OF SUMER
The Sacred Marriage Rite

The people of Sumer assemble in the palace,
The house which guides the land.
The king builds a throne for the queen of the palace.
He sits beside her on the throne.

In order to care for the life of all the lands,
The exact first day of the month is closely examined,
And on the day of the disappearance of the moon,
On the day of the sleeping of the moon,
The *me* are perfectly carried out
So that the New Year's Day, the day of rites,
May be properly determined,
And a sleeping place be set up for Inanna.

had complicated
system to determine
when New Year
was

The people cleanse the rushes with sweet-smelling cedar oil, *✓ reeds*
They arrange the rushes for the bed.
They spread a bridal sheet over the bed. *made beds out of rushes (reeds)*
A bridal sheet to rejoice the heart,
A bridal sheet to sweeten the loins,
A bridal sheet for Inanna and Dumuzi.

The queen bathes her holy loins,
Inanna bathes for the holy loins of Dumuzi,
She washes herself with soap.
She sprinkles sweet-smelling cedar oil on the ground.

The king goes with lifted head to the holy loins,
Dumuzi goes with lifted head to the holy loins of Inanna.
He lies down beside her on the bed.
Tenderly he caresses her, murmuring words of love:
"O my holy jewel! O my wondrous Inanna!"

After he enters her holy vulva, causing the queen to rejoice,
After he enters her holy vulva, causing Inanna to rejoice,
Inanna holds him to her and murmurs:
"O Dumuzi, you are truly my love."

The king bids the people enter the great hall.
The people bring food offerings and bowls.
They burn juniper resin, perform laving rites,
And pile up sweet-smelling incense.

The king embraces his beloved bride,
Dumuzi embraces Inanna.
Inanna, seated on the royal throne, shines like daylight.
The king, like the the sun, shines radiantly by her side.
He arranges abundance, lushness, and plenty before her.
He assembles the people of Sumer.

The musicians play for the queen:
They play the loud instrument which drowns out the southern storm,
They play the sweet *algar*-instrument, the ornament of the palace,
They play the stringed instrument which brings joy to all people,
They play songs for Inanna to rejoice the heart.

The king reaches out his hand for food and drink,
Dumuzi reaches out his hand for food and drink.

The palace is festive. The king is joyous.
In the pure clean place they celebrate Inanna in song.
She is the ornament of the assembly, the joy of Sumer!

The people spend the day in plenty.
The king stands before the assembly in great joy.
He hails Inanna with the praises of the gods and the assembly:
"Holy Priestess! Created with the heavens and earth,
Inanna, First Daughter of the Moon, Lady of the Evening!
I sing your praises."

My Lady looks in sweet wonder from heaven.
The people of Sumer parade before the holy Inanna.
The Lady Who Ascends into the Heavens, Inanna, is radiant.
Mighty, majestic, radiant, and ever youthful—
To you, Inanna, I sing!

COMMENTARIES

SUMERIAN HISTORY, CULTURE AND LITERATURE

by Samuel Noah Kramer

History

Sumer, the land inhabited by the ancient Sumerians, is situated in the southern half of modern Iraq, in the alluvial valleys of the Tigris and Euphrates rivers, roughly between modern Baghdad and the Persian Gulf, an area of approximately 10,000 square miles. Its climate is hot and dry, its soil is wind-swept, it has no minerals and very little stone and timber—an unpromising land seemingly doomed to poverty and desolation. But the Sumerians were a gifted, energetic, innovative people, technologically inventive and ideologically resourceful, and with the help of irrigation and a relatively pragmatic view of life and its mysteries, they turned this deprived land into a veritable Garden of Eden.

It was in Sumer that the first great urban centers came into being, and it was in these cities that the cuneiform system of writing was developed through the centuries, to spread all over the ancient Near East—witness most recently the cuneiform tablets discovered at far-away Ebla in northwest Syria. Sumerian ideas, techniques, and achievements in the areas of religion, education, literature, and law left a deep impression on their neighbors, and to some extent even on the culture of modern Western man. In more than one respect, Sumer may justifiably be designated the "cradle of civilization."

Sumer—or rather, the land that came to be known as Sumer in about 3000 B.C.—was first settled during the fifth millennium B.C., by a people speaking an unknown language that has left its traces in the names of places and occupations. Archaeologists now generally designate this people as Ubaidians, a name derived from Ubaid, an ancient *tell*, or mound, not far from the city of Ur, where the first archaeological remains of the people were uncovered. It was the Ubaidians who established the village settlements that gradually developed into Sumer's great urban centers: Ur, Eridu, Adab, Isin, Larsa, Kullab-Uruk, Lagash, Nippur, Kish. The Ubaidians were responsible for Sumer's earliest cultural advances: they were its first farmers, cattle-raisers, fishermen, weavers, leather workers, woodworkers, smiths, potters, and masons. But the Ubaidians did not long remain the sole and dominant group in the land. As their settlements prospered and flourished, they were infiltrated and invaded by Semitic nomads from the Syrian and Arabian desert lands, and it was these Semites who became the politically dominant group. For according to later Sumerian tradition, the first dynasty that reigned in Sumer following the legendary Flood was that of the city of Kish in the north, many of whose rulers bore Semitic names.

The Sumerians, on the other hand, did not arrive in the land until the second half of the fourth millennium B.C. The location of their original home is unknown, but since the Sumerian language is an agglutinative tongue like that of the Turkic peoples, it seems likely that it may have been somewhere in south-central Asia. There is also some evidence that on their way to southern Mesopotamia they may have settled for a time in western Iran. No matter where the Sumerians came from, and whatever type of culture they brought with them, this much is certain: their arrival led to an extraordinary ethnic and cultural fusion with the native population that brought about a major creative spurt for the history of civilization.

In the course of the centuries that followed, Sumer reached new heights of political power and economic wealth, and witnessed some of its most significant achievements in the arts and crafts, in monumental architecture, in religious and ethical thought, in oral myth, epic, and hymn. The Sumerian language became the prevailing tongue of the land; the cuneiform system of writing gradually developed into an effective tool of communication; and the first steps were taken for the introduction of a formal system of education.

Sumerian political history is dominated by the institution of kingship. Originally, political power lay in the hands of the free citizens and a city governor known as the *ensi*, who was no more than a peer among peers. In cases of decisions vital to the community, these free citizens met together in a bicameral assembly consisting of an upper house of "elders" and a lower house of younger fighting men. As the struggle between the various Sumerian city-states grew more violent and bitter, and as the pressures from the barbaric peoples to the east and west intensified, military leadership became an urgent need, and the king—or as he is known in Sumerian, the *lugal*, "big man"—came to the fore. At first the king was probably selected and appointed by the assembly at critical moments for specific military tasks. But gradually kingship with all its privileges and prerogatives became a hereditary institution. The king established a regular army with the chariot as the main offensive weapon, and a heavily armed infantry that attacked in phalanx formation. Sumer's victories and conquests were due largely to its superiority in military weapons, tactics, organization, and leadership.

116

The first ruler of Sumer whose deeds are recorded, if only in the briefest kind of statement, is a King of Kish by the name of Etana, who probably reigned at the very beginning of the third millennium B.C. In the Sumerian "Kinglist"—a document written centuries later—he is described as the "man who brought stability to all the lands," and it may thus be inferred that he held sway not only over Sumer but also over Sumer's neighbors.

In the course of time the power of Kish waned, and it went down to defeat at the hands of Uruk, a city in central Sumer. Some of the rulers of the Uruk dynasty, men like Enmerkar, Lugalbanda, Gilgamesh, and perhaps Dumuzi, performed such prodigious deeds of bravery and conquest that they inspired the Sumerian bards to compose epic lays characteristic of what is commonly known as a heroic age, such as that of the Greeks and Teutons much later. But despite these feats of bravery and heroism, the Uruk dynasty, too, came to a disastrous end: it was vanquished by Mesannepadda, an ambitious and power-hungry ruler of Ur, a city in southern Sumer that in biblical times came to be known as Ur of the Chaldees.

The bitter tri-partisan struggle for domination between Kish, Uruk, and Ur so weakened Sumer and so impaired its military might that for a considerable period of time it came under foreign rule. Finally, soon after the beginning of the second half of the third millennium (about 2350 B.C.), a city in southeastern Sumer by the name of Lagash, which had played no significant political role in earlier days, emerged as the dominant power in the land. The Lagash dynasty lasted less than a century, and is memorable not so much for its political and military achievements as for its archivists and men of letters, who produced the first significant contemporary historical and sociological documents in man's recorded history.

In the centuries that followed, Sumer suffered two humiliating defeats. The first was at the hands of a Semitic ruler by the name of Sargon, who conquered not only Sumer but most of western Asia. He established his capital in Agade (biblical Akkad), a city not far from Kish, and Sumer gradually became known by the hyphenated name Sumer-Akkad. Moreover, during the reign of the Akkad dynasty, the Semitic tongue now generally designated as Akkadian began to rival Sumerian as the living language of the land.

Sargon's grandson Naram-Sin, for some unknown reason, attacked Nippur, Sumer's most holy city, and desecrated and plundered its most sacred shrine. This sacrilegious act, according to the later Sumerian mythographers, led to Sumer's second catastrophic disaster: it was overrun and desolated by the Gutians, a barbarous people inhabiting the mountains of western Iran. Communication by land or sea became impossible throughout Sumer and famine ravaged the country and its people.

Toward the very end of this disastrous, humiliating period in Sumerian

117

history, the city of Lagash once again came to the fore as a political force, especially under the rule of an extraordinary and pious *ensi* named Gudea. A considerable number of inscribed statues of this ruler, originally set up in the temples of Lagash and unearthed by French excavators, have made Gudea's the Sumerian face best known to the modern world. The source and extent of his political power are as yet unknown, but his inscriptions indicate that he had trade contacts in virtually all the known world of the time. He obtained gold from Anatolia and Egypt, silver from the Taurus, cedars from the Amanus, copper from the Zagros ranges, diorite from Ethiopia, and timber from the as yet unidentified land of Dilmun.

Not long after Gudea's reign, Sumer freed itself from the Gutian yoke, and a king by the name of Ur-Nammu founded a dynasty at the city of Ur, the so-called Third Dynasty of Ur (approximately 2050–1950 B.C.), that gave promise of an impressive renaissance. Ur-Nammu was not only a capable and energetic military leader but also an outstanding social reformer and lawgiver. He promulgated the first law code in recorded history, a document whose preamble boasts that he, Ur-Nammu, removed the "chiselers" and grafters from the land, established and regulated honest weights and measures, and saw to it "that the orphan did not fall a prey to the wealthy, that the widow did not fall a prey to the powerful, that the man of one shekel did not fall a prey to the man of one mina [sixty shekels]."

Ur-Nammu was followed on the throne by his son Shulgi, who turned out to be one of the most distinguished and illustrious kings of ancient times. He was an outstanding military leader, a punctilious administrator, an energetic builder, and a lavish patron of the arts, particularly of literature and music— he claims to have established major Sumerian schools at Nippur and at Ur. The Sumerian poets and men of letters outdid themselves in composing hymns of exaltation and glorification in his honor, and these portray him as a combination of sage, soldier, sportsman, diviner, diplomat, patron of learning; a happy, optimistic king, who provided all good things for the land and its people.

Shulgi reigned for close to half a century. He was followed on the throne by his two sons, who ruled nine years each, and barely managed to keep the nation united and independent. When Shulgi's grandson, the pious and trusting Ibbi-Sin, came to the throne, he found himself under attack by Elamites and nomadic Amorites from the west, and betrayed by his own governors and generals. Finally, in the twenty-fifth year of his reign, the Elamites attacked and destroyed Ur, carrying off its king into captivity. The catastrophe made an indelible impression on the poets of Sumer, who over the years composed a whole series of mournful laments bemoaning the bitter, cruel fate that befell their land and its people.

In the centuries that followed the fall of Ur there was again a bitter

118

three-cornered struggle for dominance in the land, this time between the cities of Isin, Larsa, and Babylon. Finally, in about 1750 B.C., Hammurabi, King of Babylon, defeated Rin-Sin, King of Larsa, and emerged as the sole ruler of Sumer-Akkad. This date may be said to mark the end of ancient Sumer and the beginning of Babylonia. By this time the Sumerian people, that is, the people who spoke the Sumerian language, were virtually extinct, and the Semites were in full control. The kings were all Semites, and the spoken language was now the Semitic Akkadian. The culture as a whole, however, remained predominantly Sumerian in form and content, and the schools and academies of the land continued to use the Sumerian language and literature as the basis of their curriculum throughout the millennium.

Culture

Sumerian society was essentially urban in character, though it rested on an agricultural rather than an industrial base. In the third millennium B.C. Sumer consisted of a dozen or so city-states, each comprising a large and usually walled city surrounded by villages and hamlets. According to Sumerian religious belief, the city belonged to its ruling deity, so the outstanding feature of each city was the main temple. This largest and tallest building was situated on a high terrace, which gradually developed into a massive stage tower, or *ziggurat,* Sumer's most memorable contribution to religious architecture. The temple consisted of a rectangular central shrine, or *cella,* surrounded on its long sides by a number of rooms utilized by the priests and priestesses. In the *cella* was a niche for the deity's statue, fronted by an altar or offering table made of brick.

The temple was constructed of unattractive mud bricks, so the Sumerian architects livened up the walls by adding regularly placed buttresses and recesses. They also introduced the mud-brick column and half-column, which they decorated with colored patterns of zigzags, lozenges, and triangles by inserting thousands of painted clay cones into the mud plaster. Sometimes the inner walls of the shrine were painted with frescoes of human and animal figures, as well as a varied assortment of geometric motifs.

Although, in theory, the whole city belonged to the main god, in practice, the temple corporation owned only some of the land, which it rented out to sharecroppers. The remainder of the land was the private property of individual citizens: farmers and cattle-breeders, boatmen and fishermen, merchants and scribes, doctors and architects, masons and carpenters, smiths, jewelers, and potters. At the very top of the social hierarchy were the nobles: the palace courtiers and temple administrators, whose families owned large estates tended by clients and slaves. But even some of the poorer citizens managed to own farms and gardens, houses and cattle. Riches and poverty, success and failure were, at least to some extent, the result of private enterprise and individual drive. The more capable and industrious of the farmers, artisans, and craftsmen sold their products in the town market, receiving payment either in kind or in "money," which consisted usually of a disk or ring of silver of standard weight. Traveling merchants carried on a thriving trade from city to city, as well as with surrounding countries, both overland and by sea, and many of these tradesmen were private individuals rather than palace or temple representatives.

The economic and social life of Sumer was characterized by the all-pervading concepts of law and justice. Significant economic and legal reforms were introduced as early as the twenty-fourth century B.C. by the Lagash ruler Urukagina. Law codes were promulgated as early as the twenty-first century, and one of these, the Ur-Nammu law code, has been recovered in part. Sumerian legal documents have been excavated in large numbers: contracts, deeds, wills, promissory notes, receipts, and actual court decisions that became legal precedents. In theory, it was the king who was responsible for the administration of law and justice; in practice, the city governor or his repre-sentative, the *mashkim,* attended to the administrative and legal details. Court cases were usually heard by tribunals of three or four judges. Suits could be brought either by private parties or by the government. Evidence was taken in the form of statements from witnesses and experts, or was obtained from written documents. Oath-taking played a considerable role in court procedure.

Slavery was a recognized institution of Sumerian society. The temples, palaces, and rich estates owned slaves and exploited them for their own ben-efit. Many slaves were prisoners of war; these were not necessarily foreigners, but could be Sumerians, from a defeated neighboring city. Slaves were also recruited in other ways: freemen might be reduced to slavery as punishment for certain offenses; parents could sell their children as slaves in time of need; or a man might turn over his entire family to creditors in payment of a debt, but for no longer than three years.

The slave was the property of his master. He could be branded and flogged, and was severely punished if he attempted to escape. He did have certain legal rights, however: he could engage in business, borrow money, and buy his freedom. If a slave, male or female, married a free person, the children were free. The sale price of slaves varied with the market and the quality of the individual for sale. The average price for a grown man was ten shekels, which at times was less than the price of an ass.

The basic unit of Sumerian society was the family. Marriage was arranged by the parents. The betrothal was legally recognized as soon as the groom presented a gift to the bride's father, although it was often made binding with a contract inscribed on a tablet. While marriage was thus reduced to a practical arrangement, surreptitious premarital lovemaking was by no means unknown. The woman in Sumer had certain important legal rights: she could hold property, engage in business, and qualify as a witness. But the husband could divorce her on relatively light grounds; and if she had borne him no children, he could take a second wife. Children were under the absolute authority of their parents, who could disinherit them or even sell them into slavery. But usually children were loved and cherished; and at the parents' death, they inherited all property. Adopted children were not uncommon, and these too were treated with care and consideration—they were a kind of insurance for old age.

It is difficult to estimate with any reasonable degree of exactness the size of the population of the Sumerian cities. The number probably varied between 10,000 and 50,000. We know that, except for a few broad boulevards and public squares, the streets were narrow, winding, quite irregular, with high blank house-walls on either side. They were unpaved and undrained, and all traffic was either by foot or donkey. The average Sumerian home was a small one-story mud-brick structure consisting of several rooms grouped around an open court. The well-to-do Sumerian, on the other hand, probably lived in a two-story house of about a dozen rooms, built of brick and plastered and whitewashed both inside and out. The ground floor consisted of a reception room, kitchen, lavatory, servants' quarters, and sometimes even a private chapel. For furniture there were low tables, high-backed chairs, and wooden-framed beds. Household vessels were made of clay, stone, copper, and bronze; baskets and chests were of reed and wood. Floors and walls were adorned with reed mats, skin rugs, and woolen hangings.

The family mausoleum was often located below the house, though in early times there were special cemeteries for the dead outside the city. The Sumerians believed that the souls of the dead traveled to the underworld, and that life continued there in some way as on earth; they therefore buried with the dead their pots, tools, weapons, and jewels. Some of the earlier kings even had their courtiers, servants, and attendants buried with them, as well as their chariots with the onagers still yoked to them. It is largely from the rich tomb finds that the modern archaeologist has learned so much about the material culture of the ancient Sumerians.

In the field of art, the Sumerians were noted for their sculpture, which in early times (approximately 2600 B.C.) was abstract and impressionistic. The temple statues of those days show profound emotional and spiritual intensity, but little skill in modeling. The later sculptors were technically superior, yet their images lacked the original inspiration and vigor. Sumerian craftsmen also

121

manifested considerable skill in carving figures on stelae and plaques, vases and bowls.

It is from Sumerian sculpture and carving that we learn a good deal about the physical appearance of the Sumerians and their dress. The men were either clean-shaven or had heavy beards and long hair parted in the middle. They wore a kind of flounced skirt covered sometimes by a long cloak of felt. In later days, the "chiton" or long shirt took the place of the flounced skirt; covering this shirt was a large fringed shawl, which was carried over the left shoulder, leaving the right arm free. Women wore long dresses that resembled tufted shawls and covered them from head to foot, leaving only the right shoulder bare. Their hair was usually parted in the middle and braided into a heavy "pigtail," which was wound around the head. On important occasions elaborate headdresses were worn, consisting of ribbons, beads, and pendants.

One of the most original art contributions of the Sumerians was the cylinder seal, a small cylindrically shaped stone engraved with a design that became clear and meaningful when rolled over a clay tablet or the clay sealing of a container. The earliest cylinder seals are carefully carved gems incised with such scenes as the king on the battlefield, the shepherd defending his cattle from wild beasts, rows of animals, or hybrid creatures and monsters. Many of the later seals depicted imaginative mythological scenes, though it is often difficult to penetrate their meaning. Finally, one particular design became predominant: the "presentation" scene, in which a worshipper is being presented to a deity or a deified king. The cylinder seal became a Sumerian trademark that penetrated Anatolia, Egypt, Cyprus, and Greece.

Music, both instrumental and vocal, played a great role in Sumerian life, and some of the musicians became important figures in temple and court. Beautifully constructed harps and lyres have been excavated in the royal tombs of Ur. Percussion instruments such as the drum and tambourine were quite common, as were pipes of both reed and metal. Poetry and song flourished in the Sumerian schools. Although virtually all the recovered texts are hymns to gods and kings, there is little doubt that music, song, and dance were a major source of entertainment both at home and in the marketplace.

Sumerian religious faith and practice were based on a cosmology and theology evolved by their thinkers and sages in the early third millennium B.C. that became the basic creed and dogma of the entire Near East. The Sumerians believed that sea and water surrounded the universe on all sides; they therefore concluded that a primeval sea had existed from the beginning of time, and was a kind of "first cause" and "prime mover." In this primeval sea the universe was engendered, consisting of a vaulted heaven superimposed over a flat earth and united with it. In between, separating heaven from earth, was the moving, expanding atmosphere. Out of this airy atmosphere were fashioned the luminous bodies: the moon, the sun, the planets, and the stars. Following the separation of heaven and earth and the creation of the astral bodies, animal and human life came into existence.

This universe, so the Sumerians believed, was under the watchful charge of a pantheon, consisting of a large group of living beings. Human in form but superhuman in nature and powers, these beings, although invisible to mortal eyes, guided and controlled the cosmos in accordance with well-laid plans and duly prescribed laws. There were gods in charge of heaven, earth, air, and water; of the sun, the moon, and the planets; of wind, storm, and tempest; of the rivers, the mountains, and the steppes; of cities and states; of fields and farms; of the pickax, the brickmold, and the plow.

The leading deities of this pantheon were the four creating gods controlling the four major components of the universe: the Sky God An; the Earth Goddess Ki, whose name was changed in the course of time to Ninhursag, Queen of the Mountain; the Air God Enlil, who gradually became the leader of the pantheon; and the Water God Enki, who also came to be designated the God of Wisdom. Among the other more important deities were the Moon God Nanna; his son, the Sun God Utu; and his daughter Inanna, the Goddess of the Morning and Evening Star, known to the Semites as Ishtar. There was also a group of sky gods known as Anunna, some of whom seem to have fallen from grace and to have been carried off to the underworld.

The power of creation of the four leading deities, according to the Sumerian theologians, consisted primarily of the divine word. All the creator had to do was to make his or her plans, utter the word, and pronounce the name. Moreover, to keep the cosmic entities and cultural phenomena operating continuously and harmoniously without conflict and confusion, they devised the *me*—that set of universal and immutable rules and limits which had to be observed by god and man alike.

As for man, the Sumerians tended to take a tragic view of his fate and destiny. They were convinced that man was fashioned from clay and created for one purpose only: to serve the gods by supplying them with food, drink, and shelter so that they might have leisure for their divine activities. Life, according to the sages, was beset with uncertainty and haunted by insecurity. No one could know the destiny decreed for him by the unpredictable gods. When a person died, the spirit descended to the dark, dreary nether world, where "life" was but a dismal reflection of earthly existence.

The Sumerians, according to their own records, cherished goodness and truth, law and order, freedom and justice, mercy and compassion—and abhorred their opposites. The gods, too, preferred the ethical and the moral to the unethical and the immoral. Unfortunately, in their inscrutable fashion, they had created sin, evil, suffering, and misfortune, and there was little that

123

could be done about it. The proper course for a Sumerian Job to pursue was not to complain and argue, but to plead, lament, and wail, tearfully confessing his sins and failings. And since the great gods were far away in the distant sky and might have more important matters to attend to, the Sumerian theologians evolved the notion that each individual, or at least each head of a family, had a special personal god, a kind of good angel, who would hear his prayer and through whom he would find his salvation.

While private devotion and personal piety were important, it was the public rites and rituals that played the dominant role in Sumerian religion. The center of the cult was naturally the temple, with its priests and priestesses, its musicians and singers, its castrates and hierodules. Here sacrifices were offered daily to the gods: vegetable and animal foods, and libations of water, beer, and wine. In addition, there were the New Moon Feast and other less known monthly celebrations. Most important was the prolonged New Year celebration, culminating in the sacred marriage rite: the marriage ceremony of the reigning monarch to Inanna, the Goddess of Love and Procreation, which was believed to ensure the fertility of the soil and the fecundity of the womb.

This royal holy marriage ceremony was but one of a number of more mystical Sumerian cult practices revolving about the notion of a "dying god" and his resurrection, which served to explain, at least to some extent, two disturbing theological inconsistencies. The first concerned the bitter and incontrovertible fact that all vegetable and animal life languished to the point of death in the hot, parched summer months. This led the theologians to conclude that the god in charge had "died," that he had been carried off to the underworld, where he remained during the hot summer months, and that he did not return to the earth until the autumnal equinox, the time of the Sumerian New Year, when his sexual reunion with his wife made fields and farms, steppes and meadows, bloom and blossom once again. The second inconsistency revolved about the death of the king who had come to be deified and therefore immortal. This was resolved by identifying the king with the Vegetation God, whose annual death, resurrection, and reunion with his spouse were accepted doctrine. Every New Year, therefore, the Sumerians celebrated with pomp and ceremony, with music and song, the sacred marriage between the king as the risen god and the goddess who was his wife.

The origin and evolution of this remarkable fusion of myth and ritual, of cult and credo, are obscure. There were quite a number of "dying gods" in ancient Sumer; but the best known is Dumuzi, the biblical Tammuz, whom the women of Jerusalem were still mourning in the days of the prophet Ezekiel. Originally, the god Dumuzi was a mortal Sumerian ruler, whose life and death had made a profound impression on the Sumerian thinkers and mythographers. His wife was the ambitious, aggressive Goddess of Love, Inanna, who

124

according to the Sumerian theologians and mythographers had her insensitive, ungrateful spouse carried off to the underworld but then repented and decided that he could arise and return to earth every half year. It was this annual marriage of the king as the resurrected Dumuzi, to the goddess Inanna, that was commemorated and celebrated every New Year in the *hieros gamos* ritual.

Literature

Probably the most important Sumerian contribution to civilization was the invention and development of the cuneiform, or wedge-shaped, system of writing, which was borrowed first by the Akkadians and then by most, if not all, the surrounding peoples. The script began as a series of pictographic signs, devised by temple priests and administrators for the purpose of keeping account of the temples' resources and economic activities. In the course of the centuries, the Sumerian scribes and teachers so modified, molded, and conventionalized the script that it altogether lost its pictographic character, becoming a purely phonetic system of writing in which each sign stood for one or more syllables.

Clay tablets inscribed in cuneiform by means of a reed stylus have been excavated by the tens of thousands in the ancient buried cities of Sumer, and are now located in museums the world over. The vast majority are economic, legal, and administrative documents. But some five to six thousand tablets and fragments are inscribed with Sumerian literary works current in the early second millennium B.C. These reveal the religious beliefs, ethical ideals, and spiritual aspirations of the Sumerians, and to some extent of the ancient world as a whole.

Many of the Sumerian literary tablets and fragments were excavated toward the end of the last century; but they remained largely unpublished and unavailable to the scholarly world, and it was thus impossible to evaluate the nature and scope of their contents. In the course of the past fifty years virtually all the extant Sumerian literary pieces have been published or are in the process of being published, and quite a number of cuneiformists, young and old, have devoted much time and labor to their translation and interpretation. As a result, it is now evident that Sumerian literature comprises some twenty myths, nine epic tales, more than two hundred hymns of diverse types and genres, a considerable number of laments and dirges, several legendary historiographic documents, and a large, diversified group of "wisdom" texts, including essays, disputations, proverbs, precepts, and fables.

This vast literature, consisting of more than thirty thousand lines of text, mostly in poetic form, constitutes the oldest written literature of significant quantity and variety so far uncovered, and its recovery and restoration represent one of the major contributions of our century to the humanities. Not only is the material of immense value for its own sake, as the creative product of the Sumerian imagination, but it is also proving to be a rich treasure of prime sources for the historian of literature and religion, the biblical and classical scholar, the anthropologist and sociologist. Moreover, there is reasonable hope that this ancient treasure will be enlarged and enriched in future days. The literary compositions uncovered to date are but a fraction of those that existed in Sumer. Many a text is still lying buried in the *tells* of southern Iraq, awaiting the lucky spade of the future excavator.

Sumer, its rise and fall, provides the historian with the most ancient example of the poignant irony inherent in man's fate. As the Sumerian literary documents make amply manifest, it was the competitive drive for superiority and preeminence, for victory, prestige, and glory, that provided the psychological motivation sparking the material and cultural advances for which the Sumerians are justifiably noted: large-scale irrigation, technological invention, monumental architecture, writing, education, and literature. Sad to say, this very passion for competition and success carried within it the seed of destruction and decay.

In the course of the centuries, Sumer became a "sick society" with deplorable failings and distressing shortcomings: it yearned for peace and was constantly at war; it professed such ideals as justice, equity, and compassion, but abounded in injustice, inequality, and oppression; materialistic and shortsighted, it unbalanced the ecology essential to its economy; it was afflicted by a generation gap between parents and children, and between teachers and students. And so Sumer came to a cruel, tragic end, as one melancholy Sumerian bard bitterly laments: Law and order ceased to exist; cities, houses, stalls, and sheepfolds were destroyed; rivers and canals flowed with bitter waters; fields and steppes grew nothing but weeds and "wailing plants." The mother cared not for her children, nor the father for his spouse, and nursemaids chanted no lullabies at the crib. No one trod the highways and the roads; the cities were ravaged and their people were killed by the mace or died of famine. Finally, over the land fell a calamity "undescribable and unknown to man."

126

THE DISCOVERY AND DECIPHERMENT OF "THE DESCENT OF INANNA"

by Samuel Noah Kramer

"The Descent of Inanna"—a myth in whose recovery and restoration I played a key role—consists of more than four hundred lines of text in almost perfect condition that were pieced together from thirty tablets and fragments as a result of contributions by numerous scholars, dead and alive, young and old. The process of scholarly cooperation that began more than a century ago is only now bearing fruit.

The majority of the tablets and fragments on which "The Descent" was inscribed by the ancient mythographers sometime around 1750 B.C. lay buried and forgotten for close to four thousand years in the ruins of Nippur, Sumer's spiritual and cultural center. There they were discovered and excavated in the course of four grueling campaigns conducted by a University of Pennsylvania expedition between the years 1889 and 1900, the first American institution to excavate in the Near East.

But the excavation of the tablets and fragments was only the initial step in the process of recovering "The Descent." Once excavated, they had to be read—at least in a tentative, preliminary way—by some cuneiformist, and identified as belonging to the myth. After identification, the various texts inscribed on the individual pieces, which often duplicate and overlap each other, had to be pieced together and dovetailed into a connected text that was uniform and consistent. Then, finally, came the difficult and at times heart-breaking task of translation and interpretation.

Moreover, in the case of the Nippur tablets there was an added and rather burdensome complication: upon excavation, these tablets were divided between two museums thousands of miles apart. Not infrequently the breaks and gaps on the tablets of one of the museums could not be filled and restored without the relevant pieces in the other. Which brings us to the rather unusual and felicitous "tale of two museums": the long-lasting, uninterrupted scholarly cooperation between the Istanbul Museum of the Ancient Orient by the

The fourteen tablets and fragments shown here graphically illustrate the process of piecing together the tablets and fragments utilized in the reconstruction and decipherment of "The Descent."

Bosphorus and the University Museum of the University of Pennsylvania by the Schuylkill.

In the years 1889–1900 when the Nippur excavations took place, modern Iraq, whose southern half corresponds to ancient Sumer, was part of the Turkish empire. All the archaeological finds at Nippur—it was agreed between the American excavators and the Turkish officials—were to be divided into approximately equal halves, one half going to Istanbul, which was then the capital of the Turkish empire, while the other half became the property of the University of Pennsylvania, which had sponsored the expedition. At the time of the excavations, therefore, the thousands of clay tablets emerging from the ground, no matter what their condition (and the majority were quite fragmentary) were boxed, crated, and transported either to Philadelphia, where they were placed in the newly founded University Museum, or to Istanbul, where they were housed in the newly established Museum of the Ancient Orient.

It was only in later years that scholars began to study and identify the contents of these boxes, and it was not until 1914 that the first five pieces, inscribed with "The Descent of Inanna," were published. Two of these were in Istanbul. They were copied by Stephen Langdon, an enthusiastic, energetic, but rather careless scholar, and published in his book *Historical and Religious Texts from the Temple Library of Nippur.* The other three were in Philadelphia; they were superbly autographed by Arno Poebel and published in his *Historical and Grammatical Texts.*

But although five pieces inscribed with portions of "The Descent" were now available, their contents remained quite obscure and unintelligible, due primarily to the fragmentary nature of the tablets and the numerous breaks in text. Moreover, each of these pieces contained only a small part of the myth and it was impossible to make reasonably trustworthy connected sense of their contents. It was not until 1937, almost a quarter of a century after their publication, that the first half of "The Descent" could be reconstructed—at least partially. And although I prepared and published the relevant study in the French journal *Revue d'assyriologie et d'archéologie orientale* under the title "Inanna's Descent to the Nether World: The Sumerian Version of Ishtar's Descent," much of the credit belongs to Edward Chiera, one of the leading cuneiformists of his day.

Chiera during most of the 1920s was a member of the Oriental Department of the University of Pennsylvania; he dedicated much of his time and labor to studying, identifying and copying the Nippur literary documents. In 1923, he traveled as Crozer Fellow to Istanbul, where he copied fifty of the documents in the Museum of the Ancient Orient. These were published the very next year in his book *Sumerian Religious Texts.* Upon his return to Philadelphia, he spent the next three years copying close to three hundred Sumerian literary pieces from the Nippur collection of the University Museum. Before he could prepare them for actual printing and publication, however, he was invited by the eminent Egyptologist and historian Henry Breasted, then director of the Oriental Institute of the University of Chicago, to become editor-in-chief of its invaluable Assyrian Dictionary project.

In 1927, Chiera left Philadelphia for his new post in Chicago, carrying with him his precious copies, which the Oriental Institute undertook to publish in two volumes whenever he had prepared the introductions and plate arrangements. Unfortunately, he died suddenly and unexpectedly before he was able to complete the work. His copies, together with the relevant notes and comments, now orphaned and stranded, were turned over to me to edit for publication.[1]

Chiera's copies of the Nippur literary tablets in the University Museum included three that belonged to "Inanna's Descent" and helped to fill a good many of the gaps and breaks in its first hundred lines. But more important still, while studying and identifying the Nippur literary tablets in the University Museum, Chiera found a large fragment consisting of the lower half of a four-column tablet whose upper half had been first copied and published by Stephen Langdon in 1914. Evidently the tablet had been broken in two, either in ancient times or during the excavations, and the upper part had come to Istanbul while the lower part found its way to Philadelphia. It was Chiera's long-distance joining of this four-column tablet (two on the obverse and two on the reverse) that made it possible for me to place all the other published pieces in their proper order, and so reconstruct the text of close to three hundred lines, even though many of these were still full of crucial breaks and gaps.

The second significant publication of "The Descent" appeared in 1942, in the *Proceedings of the American Philosophical Society*.[2] In the years 1937–39, after leaving the Oriental Institute, I traveled to Istanbul as a Guggenheim Fellow and copied more than 150 tablets and fragments from the Nippur

[1] I had come to the Oriental Institute in 1932 as a research assistant on the Assyrian Dictionary project. There I met Arno Poebel, who by that time had become one of the world's leading Sumerologists—his Sumerian grammar, *Grundzüge der Sumerischen Grammatik,* which appeared in 1923, was gradually being recognized as a fundamental contribution to Sumerian research. During my stay at the Oriental Institute I sat at his feet and drank in his words, and so came to be known as a promising young Sumerologist capable of preparing Chiera's posthumous volumes for publication. It was in the course of trying to understand the contents of Chiera's copies of the Nippur literary texts, which were published in 1934 by the Oriental Institute in two volumes entitled *Sumerian Epics and Myths* and *Sumerian Texts of Varied Content,* that I became "hooked" on Sumerian literature. I have since traveled from museum to museum year after year for the past forty years, seeing to it that the thousands of Sumerian literary tablets and fragments were made available to the scholarly world in one form or another.

[2] Vol. 85, pp. 293–314.

collection of the Museum of the Ancient Orient, among which were three that belonged to "Inanna's Descent." On my return to Philadelphia, I became a research associate in the Mesopotamian Section of the University Museum, and with the help of a number of grants from the American Philosophical Society began to study and catalogue all the literary tablets of its Nippur collection. In the course of this work, I identified and copied two more tablets belonging to "The Descent." This enabled me to prepare a revised version of approximately the first two thirds of the myth, ending with the passage depicting the goddess's ascending from the nether world accompanied by the bogies and harpies who had their home there. As I noted in that study: "Here all the extant source materials for 'Inanna's Descent to the Nether World' unfortunately break off. But this is not the end of the myth. It is not too much to hope that some day in the not too distant future, the pieces on which the conclusion of the story is inscribed will be discovered and deciphered."

The hope was at least partially realized in my next major publication, which appeared in the 1951 *Journal of Cuneiform Studies*,[3] entitled "Inanna's Descent to the Nether World: Continued and Revised." This study brought to light two new pieces inscribed with portions of the myth. One was a small fragment from the Nippur Collection of the Museum of the Ancient Orient, which I had copied in 1946 when I traveled to Istanbul as the annual professor of the American Schools of Oriental Studies. The other, far more important piece was an excellently preserved tablet in the Yale Babylonian Collection, inscribed with ninety-two lines of text, the last thirty of which contained an entirely new passage that carried on the story from where it had broken off in the previously known texts.

This Yale tablet had been bought decades earlier from an antique dealer, and its provenance is therefore unknown; but it may well have been Nippur. It was identified by me as belonging to "Inanna's Descent" while I was helping to catalogue the Sumerian literary tablets in the Yale Babylonian Collection. The new material in this tablet brought the story of the myth to the point where Inanna handed over her insensitive husband Dumuzi to the *galla* of the underworld—a tragic decision that caused Dumuzi to turn pale and plead with the Sun God Utu to transform him into a snake so that he might escape the demons. There the text broke off, leaving us ignorant of Utu's response and of Dumuzi's ultimate fate.

The missing dénouement of the plot was recovered in part with "Cuneiform Studies and the History of Literature," which appeared in 1963 in the *Proceedings of the American Philosophical Society*.[4] The tablets that came to the

[3]Vol. 5, pp. 1–17.
[4]Vol. 107, pp. 485–527.

The obverse and reverse of the Ur tablet inscribed with the final third of the myth

obverse

reverse

133

rescue this time were not those excavated at Nippur but at Ur, the biblical Ur of the Chaldees. Here Leonard Woolley had conducted a joint British Museum–University Museum expedition between the years 1923 and 1933, and among the thousands of tablets he excavated were four that belonged to "Inanna's Descent." They were copied in turn by the late Cyril Gadd and published in the sixth volume of *Ur Excavation Texts* (written jointly by Gadd and myself).

One of these Ur tablets consisted of a telescopic version of "Inanna's Descent" that provided us with Utu's favorable response to Dumuzi's plea: he transformed Dumuzi into a snake and thus enabled him to escape the demons. Of the other three tablets, two duplicated material already known but added some significant variants.

The third—the upper part of an unusually wide tablet—proved to be of the utmost importance. The obverse duplicated material long known; but the reverse provided the hitherto missing end of the myth. It began with Inanna's blessing of a fly that seemed to have informed her of Dumuzi's whereabouts after his escape from the *galla,* and concluded with her decree that Dumuzi must stay in the underworld only half the year and that his sister Geshtinanna would take his place for the other half. Still missing were approximately twenty lines of text depicting the events that took place between Dumuzi's escape from the demons and Inanna's Solomon-like verdict.

The publication of my 1963 study in the *Proceedings of the American Philosophical Society* marked the fourth major revision of "Inanna's Descent," whose text had been recovered and reconstructed gradually over a period of fifty years. It was high time that a new, complete variorum edition of the myth be compiled, together with a translation and interpretation that would include the relevant contributions of such eminent cuneiformists as Thorkild Jacobsen, Adam Falkenstein, and Benno Landsberger. This very useful task was performed ably and competently in 1974 by William R. Sladek in his "Dissertation submitted to the Johns Hopkins University in conformity with the requirements for the degree of Doctor of Philosophy," prepared under the expert guidance of his teacher, Jerrold S. Cooper, and of Åke Sjöberg, my successor as curator of the Tablet Collection at the University Museum.

Which brings us to the Jayne Lecture delivered by me in 1979 at the November meeting of the American Philosophical Society.[5] The lecture is entitled "Sumerian Literature and the British Museum: The Promise of the Future," and a large part of it is devoted to the Ur tablet whose upper third had been copied by Cyril Gadd and published in the sixth volume of the *Ur Excavation Texts.* The obverse of this fragment duplicated material already

[5] *Proceedings* of the American Philosophical Society Vol. 124, pp. 295–312.

known, but its reverse, as we have seen, provided us with the very end of the myth: it related that Inanna, moved by Dumuzi's tears, had decided to allow him to leave the underworld every half year, and to have his place taken by his loving, self-sacrificing sister Geshtinanna. All that was missing, therefore, was the approximately twenty-line passage immediately before this, depicting the events that befell Dumuzi after he had eluded the *galla* with Utu's help. It seemed not unreasonable to hope that, once the lower two thirds of the tablet were located, this missing passage would be recovered, and the text of "The Descent" would be virtually complete.

Sad to say, it did not turn out that way. Several years ago, the missing part of the Ur tablet was found in one of the cupboards of the British Museum, and joined to the part copied by Gadd. But as the photographs of the now almost complete tablet show, only the obverse of the new piece is fairly well preserved, and its text duplicates the lines of the myth already known from other sources. The reverse, which contained the missing passage, is very poorly preserved, and is of no help in restoring the text of approximately twenty lines. It may be surmised, of course, that these lines depicted such events as the final seizure of Dumuzi by the *galla;* the bitter lamentation of his despairing sister, Geshtinanna; and the appearance on the scene of the clever, knowing fly who informed the goddesses of Dumuzi's whereabouts. But none of this is certain, and our knowledge of what actually took place must await the future discovery of some duplicating tablet.

INTERPRETATIONS OF
INANNA'S STORIES AND HYMNS

by Diane Wolkstein

Introduction

In the first three lines of "The *Huluppu*-Tree," we meet the predominant stylistic feature of the Cycle of Inanna: repetition. Words are repeated, sentence structure is repeated; and by this slow, studied, almost hypnotic repetition we are transported into another realm—the timeless realm of the gods, the soul, and the origins of life.

All the Sumerian tales in this collection are connected to a religious foundation about which, except for the stories and hymns, we unfortunately have very little factual information. Nevertheless, we need to approach these stories as sacred narratives, spiritual explorations of the place of the gods and the human psyche in the universe. In all the stories there is a focusing on such spiritual concepts as rule, destiny, and the *me* (the sacred culture of Sumer). Much like the sculpture of the time, the Sumerian stories have a stark, raw, wide-eyed quality, as if the poet were attempting to pierce through conventions into the very essences of life in order to see "what is," to understand what it is all made of, how, and why.

Unfortunately, the Sumerian priest no longer exists to explain ambiguous terminology or explicate ritual and symbols. In addition, we do not even know at what period the stories were created; they could have been created any time between 1900 B.C. and 3500, or even further back. Yet despite, or most likely because of their sacred roots, the stories continue to have a compelling hold on us. When I have told them, the responses from the audience have been striking: "I felt as I did the first time I stepped into the cathedral at Chartres," or, "It was like going behind a mirror." And in the telling—especially in the moments of repetition such as the second or third time Inanna's story is told in "The *Huluppu*-Tree," or during the seven disrobings in "The Descent of Inanna"—I, too, have felt the strange opening-up quality of these stories, as if I were falling out of the storyteller-audience framework into a deeper, more eternal soul-place.

These commentaries have been written in response to the many questions of listeners: "Who is the *Anzu*-bird?" "Why did Inanna go to the underworld?" "Why did she sentence her husband to death?" My thoughts are in no way definitive, but rather responses to working with the material. I had to speak back. I did so, first by trying to take into consideration the Sumerian context for the symbols, both in their literary and cultural aspects, and then by relying on hunch, speculation, and a storyteller's intuition.

✾

The Huluppu-*Tree*

In the first days, in the very first days,
In the first nights, in the very first nights,
In the first years, in the very first years . . .

"The *Huluppu*-Tree" is one of the world's first recorded tales of genesis. Such a claim however, ought not to lead us to consider *first* to mean "primitive" or unformed. The art and thinking of the Sumerians and Akkadians had an enormous breadth, sophistication, and variety in its representation of the universe. The Sumerian sculptor, who wished to exalt in the very tangible delights of love, could realistically portray a woman and man embracing (See *Lovers Embracing on the Bed*, page 43). The Sumerian artist, who was searching to represent the frightening, impenetrable, and imprisoning aspects of the snake, could choose to draw his subject in a decorative, schematic manner (see *Snake with Interlacing Coil*, page 7). Similarly, the Sumerian poet, who was investigating in "the *Huluppu*-Tree" the moment of beginnings,[1] was able to create a structure which would evoke the nature of growth.

In order to penetrate the closely woven fabric of the Sumerian poet, I have approached the story from three viewpoints: that of the story's poetics, its character development, and its thematic material.

In Sumerian there is no rhyme. However, the intricate patterns of similar and alternating sounds of vowels and consonants and the similar and alternating verb and noun endings give the language a musical resonance.[2] Unfortunately, the richness of the sound play in Sumerian is not available to the non-Sumerian reader; nevertheless, we can begin to unlock this mysterious

[1]See Mircea Eliade's *Myth and Reality* (Harper & Row, 1963), for a discussion of "first times" and "beginnings."
[2]See Piotr Michalowski, "Carminative Magic: Towards an Understanding of Sumerian Poetics." Unpublished manuscript.

tale by examining it from another aspect of poetics. As Adele Berlin has explained: "The different ordering of parallel clauses within a multi-clause stanza produces many patterns . . . it is here . . . that the modern reader will find the beauty and intricacy of Sumerian poetry."[3]

The story begins with a progressive three-part parallelism:

> In the first *days,* in the very first *days,*
> In the first *nights,* in the very first *nights,*
> In the first *years,* in the very first *years . . .*

The repetition of "days" is then picked up in the fourth and fifth lines, linking them to the previous lines, yet presenting new material in a new, balancing parallelism. This balancing parallelism has the same subject:

> In *the first days* when *everything needed* was brought into being,
> In *the first days* when *everything needed* was properly nourished . . .

The same subject-balancing parallelism is continued in the sixth and seventh lines:

> When *bread* was baked in the shrines of the land,
> And *bread* was tasted in the homes of the land . . .

When, in the eighth and ninth lines, the balancing parallelism switches from the subject to the verb,

> When heaven had *moved away* from earth
> When earth had *separated* from heaven . . .

we have the reassuring sense of the growth of one thing into the other. We understand the natural order of things: one thing follows another, one thing flows out of another, until a third line is added to the balancing parallelism that contradicts the previous couplet both in subject and verb:

> And the *name of man* was *fixed.*

Previously, the story of creation had been a developing natural process: existence was set into time (lines 1–3); life's vital aspects were brought forth and nourished (lines 4–7); the oneness of the world was divided (lines 8–9). But with the tenth line, *And the name of man was fixed,* consciousness—artifice, effort, intention—begins.

With the act of naming that which is in flux, what is in movement becomes shaped and what is inside becomes manifest. To give a name is to bring into existence and recognition. In Indian mythology, Brahma created apparitions

[3]Adele Berlin, *Enmerkar and Ensuhkesdanna.* Philadelphia: The University Museum, 1979, p. 15.

from his unconscious; then the world guardian, Daksha, gave the apparitions names so that they might be known and their functions assigned to them. In Sumerian *mu-lugal* means "man's name" and also "life-giving properties." To give a name to something is to bring it into a second (and conscious) existence. The sentence, *And the name of man was fixed,* which occurs as the disruptive third part of a parallelism (consciousness always being a jarring and disturbing event), is also the tenth line in the larger story of creation and represents a new order: the conscious order of creation.

Lines 11 and 12 take up the previous repetitive verb-balancing parallelism of lines 8 and 9, suggesting a restoration of the process of creation. And now since man has been named, the gods, too, are named:

When . . . An had *carried off* the heavens,
And . . . Enlil had *carried off* the earth . . .

However, the third line of the parallelism, with its new subject and contrasting verb, once again arrests the action of the story and throws the spotlight onto the meaning of the thirteenth line:

When . . . *Ereshkigal, was given* the underworld for her domain

As in so many world mythologies, 13 is the number of death. It is the unlucky, fateful number. In lines 11 and 12, the two male gods, An and Enlil, actively take over their realms; but in line 13, the female goddess, Ereshkigal, receives her domain and her fate. And that which is assigned to Ereshkigal, the House of Death, of Darkness, of Decay, of Dust, is the same realm that awaits all of humankind. The flow of creation is brought to a halt, for though man's name has been "fixed," what purpose is there in life and awareness if it is all to be undone in the House of Decay? Who will attempt to understand death and thus to find meaning in life?

The answer to the question raised in the first section is given as the Wise One, Father Enki, the God of Wisdom, enters the story at the beginning of the second section. The progressive three-part parallelism is repeated; but this time, the action is accomplished in two rather than three lines:

He set sail; the *Father* set sail,
Enki, the God of Wisdom, set sail for the underworld.

The father who journeys to the underworld can be appreciated in two ways: metaphysically, as the "God of Wisdom," and sexually, as the God of the Waters (water also means "semen" in Sumerian). As God of Wisdom, Enki takes up humanity's quest to confront the Unknown. Like other shamanic figures who voyage to the underworld, Enki is assaulted by stones and animal spirits. He is battered and bruised by the underworld, which is possessive of

139

its realm; but he does not turn back. The battle between conscious and unconscious forces rages. As God of the Waters, Enki sets sail into the underworld, penetrating Ereshkigal, the Queen of the Underworld, who reacts by storming, throwing up stones, devouring, and roaring.

The suspense of the struggle between male and female, conscious and unconscious, is achieved grammatically by setting up one balancing parallelism after another. The entire second section is made up of parallel couplets. Whereas in the first section the balancing parallelism flows from subject to verb, here there is no varying of the balancing-subject parallelism, nor is there a movement into a three-part contrary or synthetic parallelism. The repetition of parallelisms stresses the confrontation: the two powers are equal. No resolution occurs until the third section, where the answer is given in the form of a synthesis. From the encounter between the God of Wisdom and the Queen of the Underworld, a tree comes into existence.

The third section repeats the progressive three-part parallelism of the first and second sections, but now as time is speeded up, the parallelism is contracted into the space of one line:

At that time, a *tree*, a *single tree*, a *huluppu*-tree . . .

When the third section begins, we have come through time, encountered the gods, and have arrived, with the planting of the seed, on earth. Soon Inanna enters and the plot can begin.

The dynamic contrapuntal rhythms of the structure continue throughout the story, creating a pulsating web of time. Each section both echoes and responds to the previous section. Only at the end of the first part of "The *Huluppu*-Tree," when there is a resolution to Inanna's dilemma, do the varying two- and three-part parallelisms give way to a new, four-part parallelism:

From the trunk of the tree he carved a throne for his holy sister.
From the trunk of the tree Gilgamesh carved a bed for Inanna.
From the roots of the tree she fashioned a *pukku* for her brother.
From the crown of the tree Inanna fashioned a *mikku* for Gilgamesh,
    the hero of Uruk.

The exchange between male and female, between the goddess, Inanna, and the mortal, Gilgamesh, causes a resolution and a respite to the previous regular/irregular pace of the story. Moreover, the number *four,* connected to the four directions, the square, gives a sense of grounding and completion.

A second approach to the understanding of "The *Huluppu*-Tree" is through its characters. Enki and Ereshkigal battle in the prelude; the plot begins with the *huluppu*-tree and Inanna.

The *huluppu*-tree sprouts by the Euphrates River, but soon it is struck by the South Wind and forced into the waters. If it had not been for Inanna, the tree in its untended state of nature might have perished. Inanna rescues the tree from the waters and brings it to a place of cultivation.

Only after Inanna has cared for the tree for a period of time in the enclosure of her garden do her wishes connected with it emerge. Just as in the first section,

> In the first days when everything needed was brought into being,
> In the first days when everything needed was properly nourished,

life must be properly nourished and cared for before it can take root and begin to be differentiated. From the growing tree Inanna wishes to have a shining throne and a bed.

However, in conflict with these wishes, the first fact we are told about Inanna is that she fears the "word" of An and Enlil. An, the Sky God, and Enlil, the Air God, are Sumer's lawgivers and ordainers who direct the fates of those in heaven and on earth. As Jacobsen has noted, "A command of An and Enlil is not known ever to be changed."[4] The "word" or fate awaiting the young woman Inanna is that which she wishes and also that which she fears: her throne and bed, her queenship and womanhood.

Inanna's sexual fears and wishes, which are those of all adolescents, are further amplified in the history of the relations of the gods in Inanna's family tree. (See Inanna's Family Tree, pp. x–xi.) On her mother's side there was a sense of warmth and relatedness; on her father's side, a more forced, controlled and controlling sense of relationship. Inanna's great-grandfather An, the Sky God, had mated with her great-grandmother Ki (or Urash), the Earth Goddess. Ki had given birth to trees, reeds, vegetation, and Enlil. The imperious Enlil had raped the young woman Ninlil (forcing open her too small vagina) and Nanna, the Moon God, Inanna's father, was born. Through the goddess Nammu, of the Watery Deep, An had also fathered Enki, the God of Flowing Water and Wisdom. Enki had mated with Ningikuga, the Reed Goddess, and Inanna's mother, Ningal, was born. Nanna fell in love with Ningal and she with him. It was from this joyful impetuous union that Inanna, the Morning and Evening Star, and Utu, the Sun God, were born. Inanna is thus descended from a grandmother who was raped and a grandmother and mother who were loved.

But now Inanna, who was born of divine parents, has descended to earth and waits as a "young woman" for her throne and bed. Inanna waits; but her tree does not come into the fruition she wishes. Instead it becomes the habitat of Inanna's unacknowledged, unexpressed fears and desires.

The snake, because it sloughs off its own skin, has long been connected

---

[4]Thorkild Jacobsen, Yale University Press, *The Treasures of Darkness.* New Haven and London: 1976, p. 187.

with rebirth. In the Akkadian *The Epic of Gilgamesh,* contemporary to the Cycle of Inanna, the snake steals the "flower of rebirth" from the unmindful Gilgamesh. Both because of its regenerative aspect and its phallic likeness, the appearance of the snake suggests rebirth and sexuality. Moreover, the text states that the snake "could not be charmed." Inanna will not be able to appease, tame, or disregard it. The snake is immune to the laws of the land.

The *Anzu*-bird was known to the Sumerians from the story of "Ninurta-Turtle,"[5] in which the *Anzu*-bird unsuccessfully attempts to steal the *me,* the attributes of civilization and knowledge, from Enki, the God of Wisdom. The mature *Anzu*-bird, depicted in Sumerian art with the great wings of an eagle and the face of a lion (see page 8), craves power and knowledge.

Lilith does not appear in any other Sumerian texts. To understand her nature, we need to consider various later texts. In Hebrew legend, she was the first bride of Adam; but insisting on her own equality, she refused to copulate with him, for she did not want to be underneath him. She fled from Adam and remained forever outside human relationship or regulation, possessed by an avid, insatiable sexuality. She was cursed by the daily death of a hundred of her demon children, for which she takes continual revenge by stealing, injuring, or killing human infants.[6] In Zoharic texts, she has dominion over all instinctual, natural beings, over "every living creature that creepeth." Lilith forms with the *Anzu*-bird and the snake a triad of sexual, lawless creatures who live outside the bounds of the Sumerian community and seek power only for themselves. These are Inanna's unexpressed fears and desires, which have now been "named."

Inanna had wanted a throne and bed. She had wanted the end result—her rule and womanhood. Yet the snake, the bird, and Lilith are essential to Inanna's achieving her wishes, for they give her fears an external form so that she can begin to *see* them. The three creatures embody the primitive, grasping, human aspects Inanna must recognize and let go of if she is to be deserving of the gifts of "the throne" and "the bed."

Inanna dissolves into tears at the realization of her own dark solipsistic cravings:

> The young woman who loved to laugh wept.
> How Inanna wept!

But weeping has little effect on the creatures who will not be tamed.

After intense and repetitive weeping, Inanna's own resistances weaken, and she is prepared to move to another state of awareness. At dawn, with the

[5]Bendt, Alster, *Journal Cuneiform Studies,* vol. 24, 1971–2, pp. 120ff.
[6]Louis Ginzberg, *Legends of the Bible.* Philadelphia: Jewish Publication Society of America, 1956, p. 35.

renewal of light and consciousness, she asks for help, not from her father or mother, but from her own peer group. Her divine brother, Utu, the Sun God, refuses her. Her earthly brother, Gilgamesh[7] the hero of Uruk, who functions in this story as the son of Enki, the God of Wisdom—responds to Inanna's plea.[8]

Gilgamesh enters Inanna's garden and by using the bronze ax, a cutting weapon of civilization, he defeats the untamable snake. With the death of the snake, Inanna becomes joined to Gilgamesh, who has entered her garden and released her from her fears. The bond which is formed between the solitary Inanna and the hero-king of Uruk also extends to those who have aided the king, the people of Sumer. As a sign of their new relationship, Gilgamesh and Inanna exchange gifts.

Inanna gives Gilgamesh a *pukku* and a *mikku*.[9] We read in the second part of "The *Huluppu*-Tree" (not published here)[10] that Gilgamesh loses his gifts. He does not yet have sufficient consciousness to use them wisely. His vainglorious use of the *pukku* brings bitterness, lamentation, and tears to the mothers, sisters, and young maidens of Uruk, so that the wet earth opens and the *pukku* and *mikku* are lost in the underworld.

In "The *Huluppu*-Tree" Gilgamesh is the brazen young hero, full of his manliness and the signs of his physical strength—his heavy ax, which weighs 450 pounds, and his great armor, which weighs 60 pounds. But he also acts in the role of a hero-king. He defeats lawless nature (Lilith and the beasts) by performing the same civilizing tasks as King Gilgamesh performs, when (in *The Epic of Gilgamesh*) he enters Ishtar's cedar forest, kills the monster Humbaba and then fells the trees.

Although Gilgamesh has not come into his full development in "The *Huluppu*-Tree," he is nevertheless Inanna's initiator, for he brings courage, decisiveness, and strength to Inanna in her moment of weakness. With her consent, he rids the young woman of her "creatures of the wilderness."

Inanna brought the *huluppu*-tree from its free-floating state in the wilderness into the enclosure of her garden. But without the will of the hero-king Gilgamesh, the tree can not bear "the fruit" Inanna wishes for. In order to

---

[7]Gilgamesh was said to be two-thirds god and one-third human. In the stories he is mortal and acts in a human manner. From the Family Tree it can be seen that he is of the same generation as Inanna, suggesting a brother-sister kinship relationship.

[8]Gilgamesh was considered an avatar of Dumuzi, the son of Enki. As one who is linked to Enki, Gilgamesh, in the second part of the story, parallels Enki's role in the first part of the story, by coming to the rescue of the conscious part of Inanna against the forces of the snake or the underworld.

[9]Sumerologists have not yet been able to translate the meaning of either *pukku* or *mikku*. One possible explanation is that they are emblems of kingship such as a rod or ring. See page 9 in text for illustration.

[10]For the full story of "The *Huluppu*-Tree," see S. N. Kramer, *The Sumerians: Their History, Culture, and Character.* Chicago: University of Chicago Press, 1963, pp. 199–205.

produce a throne and bed, a green tree must be changed into a hewn tree.[11] Inanna, Gilgamesh, and the tree are all in their formative stages. Because of its lawless, uncivilizable occupants, the tree—changed from benign to malevolent—must therefore be destroyed. It is with the conscious consent of Inanna and Gilgamesh that the tree is uprooted a third time. It is then brought by Gilgamesh and his companions from the garden into the city and civilization, where it bears "reciprocal gifts" for all of Sumer.

Both Inanna and Gilgamesh are enriched by the death and transformation of the tree. Inanna is now prepared to be a woman, and Gilgamesh has proven his manliness. Although they do not become united, Gilgamesh, by entering Inanna's garden is drawn closer to his feminine side. Inanna, provided with a shining bed, awaits her consort; and prepared with a throne, she is ready to act on her own.

A third approach to the story is through the major themes. The *huluppu*-tree, created at the beginning of the story, reflects the reality and struggle of the gods as well as Inanna's own psychic reality. The tree embodies the dual forces of the universe: Enki and Ereshkigal, consciousness and unconsciousness, light and darkness, male and female, and the power of life and the power of death.

The Sumerian pictograph for plant ▦ displays the complexity of the synthesis wonderfully. The two sets of four lines cross each other at right angles, forming a mesh, which is a third new entity, yet maintains the equal identities of the opposing forces.

The image of the tree as the synthesis of these numinous powers is also effectively seen in outer reality, for the tree grows from the darkness and underworld into the light and consciousness. It is anchored in the underworld and grows toward the heavens. The tree is a part of the three kingdoms: the underworld of Ereshkigal, the earth of Enlil, and the heavens of An. The wonder of the tree continues to exist today, for although we still cannot explain the mystery of the *first* seed, we can take the seed in our hand and say, here is the beginning of life. It will emerge from the underworld, strive toward the heavens, and die back into the underworld, from which one of its descendants will emerge.

The Hebrew story of creation parallels the Sumerian account of "The *Huluppu*-Tree" in many ways. In Genesis, on the first day God created time, on the second day the heavens, and on the third day the earth, "which brought forth grass, the herb-yielding seed, and the fruit-tree-yielding fruit after his

[11]See David Bynum's *The Daemon in the Wood* (Cambridge: Harvard University Press, 1978) for a discussion of the life-giving/life-withdrawing aspects of the green tree and the reciprocal, cultural aspects of the dry or hewn tree.

kind, whose seed *is* in itself." For both cultures the tree represents the first living thing on earth.

The tree also provides for both cultures a configuration of the forces of life and death and consciousness and lack of knowledge. It may be that the powers of the biblical trees in the center of the Garden of Eden, the Tree of Life and the Tree of Knowledge of Good and Evil, are based on the joined powers of the Sumerian *huluppu*-tree. In any case, the biblical Tree of Knowledge contains great powers, for God warns Adam not to eat of its fruit or he will die. When Adam and Eve both disobey ("The woman saw that the tree . . . [was] desired to make one wise"), they discover their own nakedness and sexuality and lose their opportunity for immortality. Yet they gain a knowledge of good and evil. They are then expelled from the Garden of Eden. But they do not go completely unprepared, for they go with their newly acquired consciousness. Contact with the tree, which has *within itself* its own means of regeneration, gives the partakers a chance also to be reborn, if not physically, then in stages of understanding.

When Inanna plants the *huluppu*-tree in her garden, she brings the forces of Ereshkigal and Enki into her protected retreat. The living tree, which mirrors the larger world as well as Inanna's interior world, is inhabited by creatures who each strive toward rebirth alone. Yet for Inanna, at this moment, rebirth by herself is not possible. Just as Eve shared the fruit of the Tree of Knowledge with Adam and "the eyes of both were opened," the young Inanna, also, appeals to her brothers—first Utu, then Gilgamesh.

By the time Gilgamesh enters Inanna's garden, both Inanna and we are ready for Inanna's awakening. We have lived through the story of the creating and the undoing of the universe three times (once in the outer world, with the presence of Ereshkigal, and twice in Inanna's inner world, with the presence of the frightening creatures). The balancing parallelisms have led again and again to the changing third. Stasis and anti-stasis have prepared us for the end of Inanna's maidenhood. With the cutting ax of civilization, Gilgamesh pierces the feared snake, the beast that would go forever around and around upon itself, and Inanna's projected fears disappear. The tree, freed of Inanna's demons, is brought into the city.

The tree, which was born from the confrontation of life's opposing forces, is now shared between Inanna and Gilgamesh; woman and man, goddess and mortal. Contact with the tree brings Sumerian man and woman to a closer understanding of life's forces: the world's creation and its human echo, woman's sexuality and her emerging consciousness. The sons of the city who help Gilgamesh are benefactors as well, for it is from the wood of the *huluppu*-tree that the throne and bed of their goddess is fashioned. When Inanna begins

145

her rule, she will be sitting on the throne of the *huluppu*-tree, and her understanding of life and death, consciousness and lack of consciousness, will be increased accordingly. Likewise, when she holds a man in her arms, the bed will murmur to them both the secrets of life and death, light and darkness.

Inanna and the God of Wisdom

Inanna placed the *shugurra,* the crown of the steppe, on her head.

When Inanna places the crown of the steppe on her head, she assumes her role as Queen of the Land.[12] As Queen of the Land of Sumer, Inanna is responsible to and receives her power from the resources and fertility of the land. With the *shugurra* on her head, Inanna goes to the sheepfold, which is the center of nature in Sumer. Leaning against a fruit tree, she rejoices in her own natural powers—her wondrous vulva. In Sumerian, the word for sheepfold, womb, vulva, loins, and lap is the same. The images presented in the first few lines—shepherd, sheepfold, apple tree, young woman, and vulva—are all related to fertility. Gone is the brooding, fearful adolescent girl of "The *Huluppu*-Tree." Inanna has received her throne and crown. The story of "Inanna and the God of Wisdom" begins with Inanna delighting in her womanhood and wishing to test its powers.

Inanna decides to go on a journey. Often in heroic stories, before the hero sets out on a journey, he takes up and brandishes his sword or manly weapon. In "The *Huluppu*-Tree," before the young Gilgamesh ventures into Inanna's garden, he demonstrates his extraordinary virility by raising a bronze ax weighing 450 pounds. Likewise, the young Inanna, about to set out on a journey, exults, in an amazingly straightforward way, in her feminine powers —her wondrous vulva.

Inanna sets out to visit Enki, the God of Wisdom, who is also the God of the Waters. In "The *Huluppu*-Tree," after the new world is divided, Enki appears, but he is not assigned a fixed domain. Yet without the presence on earth of Enki, the God of the Waters, no life is possible. With his presence, water, which permeates and fertilizes the land, gives the earth the power of life and creativity. This in part accounts for the dual aspect of Enki's powers, for as well as being God of the Waters, he also has many powers over the earth (in Sumerian, "Enki" means literally God of the Earth). Enki's iconographic

---

[12]In the Sumerian section of the Philadelphia University Museum an exquisite queen's crown, excavated from Ur and dated to around 2500 B.C., is on display. Unlike most European queens' crowns, which are made of solid gold embedded with precious gems, this Sumerian queen's crown is a band of lapis lazuli beads to which are sewn the earth's wonders: miniature golden fruit trees, plants, and tiny animals of many different kinds.

emblem, the goat-fish, further indicates his earth-water aspect: the goat goes to the highest point of all earth animals and the fish to the lowest depths.

The fertilizing, free-flowing, purifying, calming, and raging characteristics of waters are personified in the many roles Enki plays in Sumerian stories. He is the Creator of Humankind ("Enki and Ninmah"), the Fertilizer of the Land, and Organizer of his Creations ("Enki and the World Order"). He is a Magician and a Master of Ritual and Incantation. Rather than an upholder of the laws of the gods, he is a Mediator between Men (the debate literature) and a Mediator before the Gods on the part of the Mortals ("Atrahasis"). Always following his own feelings and instincts, Enki is the Great Shaman ("The Descent of Inanna" and "The *Huluppu*-Tree"). Enki's sacred shrine, the Abzu, is built above the regions of the underworld. His city, Eridu, is located near where the fresh and salt waters meet, where the Tigris and Euphrates rivers and the Persian Gulf converge.

When we consider the myriad aspects of the God of Wisdom, Inanna's decision to journey to Eridu can be understood as a wish to be "fertilized" by the sexual as well as the magical, spiritual, and cultural powers of life—both for herself and for her queendom. With youthful audacity, she boasts that *she* will bless Enki, the God of Wisdom. But Enki refers to Inanna as "the young woman," and bids his servant Isimud treat Inanna "as if" she were an equal. Each deity supposes superiority over the other.

As soon as Enki and Inanna begin to drink, Enki the overconfident, over-effusive host offers the treasures of his kingdom to his guest. She accepts. Enki is full of generosity; Inanna is full of intention. Gaiety surrounds them. Enki donates and Inanna takes. After Inanna itemizes the *me* she has been given, they are placed on the Boat of Heaven. Inanna's Boat of Heaven (which Inanna in "The Courtship of Inanna and Dumuzi" compares to her wondrous vulva) is of sufficient amplitude to hold all the *me*.

The ordering of the *me* offers some indication of what the Sumerians— or the Sumerian priesthood who had possession of the *me*—valued. The first eight groupings center on the priesthood and the rituals involved in serving the gods, the king, and the temple. Since the *me* are referred to as the "holy *me*," it can be inferred that the "attributes of civilization" were derived from and inspired by the gods and made available to the people through the institution of the temple and its servants. The last six groupings, beginning with "the art of the hero," are related to humanity's concerns: political power, the secure dwelling place, crafts, husbandry, emotions, the family, counseling, and decision.[13]

---

[13]By the end of the story, the *me* have been announced four times. Since there are about one hundred *me*, this method of listing the *me* four times within a story may have been an early Sumerian pedagogical technique for learning one's *"me"* in an enjoyable manner. One child who

There is a wonderful irony in the last of Enki's gifts to Inanna. When Inanna sets out for Eridu, she is eager for adventure, eager to test her powers, eager to be fertilized. During the drinking bout, she happily accepts each gift. But at the moment she receives from Enki the last gift, "the making of decisions," Inanna's eagerness turns from bravado to true decision. Inanna *decides* she wants to keep the *me;* and so she hastily and prudently departs. Although most of the *me* stress the power and importance of the priesthood and servitude, without "the making of decisions" the other *me* are meaningless. Without the individual's decision there can be no kingship, leathermaking, princess/priestess, counseling. It is the will—the strength and ability to make decisions—that houses the divine attributes. It is the will that perceives, believes, and takes action.

Adding further irony to the story, the great God of Wisdom loses his own sense of form and control through drunken frivolity. Enki, the protector of Sumer's most spiritualized treasure, the *me,* symbol of the ultimate form of things, loses his will. To understand this dual aspect of Enki—his highly differentiated standards of culture as well as his carousing, companionable frivolity—is to have a fuller view of "wisdom."

As God of Wisdom, Enki knows that the powers of knowledge need to be shared; as King of Eridu, he knows that the best rule is the self-sufficiency of his citizens; as Father, he knows that the best way to raise his children is by encouraging initiative and independence. Like the first drop of water, which generously offers a place to the second drop, Enki, in his state of drunkenness, freely shares his own powers.

Perhaps the vessel of Urash from which Enki drinks partially influences his generous state of mind. Urash, the primordial Mother of the Earth, does not hold back. In giving birth, Urash gives away everything; all that a plant or tree needs is given in the birthing. No power is withheld. But surely the beer within the vessel also contributes to Enki's fluid state. Immediate concerns, cares, and boundaries vanish. Enki's ego melts. The God of Wisdom gives to the young Queen of Uruk all the necessary knowledge for the ruling of her kingdom. Yet as soon as the drink wears off and his consciousness returns, so do Enki's possessive, jealous, and controlling aspects. Enki—god, king, father, and magician—wants his riches for himself.

Now the other side of the God of Wisdom, the dark shaman who withholds rather than gives birth, emerges, and Enki summons his occult powers. Of the six creatures who guard the treasures of Eridu, we have fragmentary

---

heard the story of the *me* told me he imagined that the *me* were loaded onto the boat in inflatable plastic containers of different shapes and sizes. They were stored in these containers; then, when a certain *me* was needed, the container was squeezed slightly to let out a little fear, kindness, or courage.

information on only two: the *enkum* and the *lahamas*.[14] The *enkum* are protective spirits created by Enki and placed under the floors and foundations of Eridu. They are part-human, part-animal, and have hair that hangs loosely behind them. The *lahamas* are dragon-like stone statues who guard the doorways of Eridu and act as messengers for Enki. Throughout world mythology, wherever there is a great treasure there are also dragons, monsters, and demons to guard that treasure. The mysteries or spiritual treasures offer abundance and riches, but only to those capable of both winning and protecting them. Enki, who has lost his treasures, sends his servant Isimud with the *enkum*-creatures to rescue the *me* of Eridu.

When Isimud requests that Inanna return the treasures she has been given, she is indignant. She rages against her father. She no longer sees him as the supportive, generous father, but as the one who withholds, insisting on his own rights and desires. In her childish eyes, her father is a tyrant, a fraud, a monstrous liar. However, when Enki's henchmen seize the Boat of Heaven, Inanna drops her attitude of deceived, dependent, naïve child. She recognizes the reality of her father's dual nature and takes action.

By summoning her own *sukkal,* Ninshubur, Inanna defends the treasures she wishes to bring to her city. Although a *sukkal* is a servant who may act in many different capacities—as vizier, minister, chancellor, messenger, general, or warrior—a *sukkal* who carries out orders often has powers superior to his or her master. Inanna's *sukkal* Ninshubur, often referred to as the servant of the holy shrine of Uruk, seems to represent the inner spiritual resources of Inanna, which are intended for the greater good of Sumer. (In other Sumerian literature Ninshubur acts as the *sukkal* of the Sky God, An—the creator and the oldest of the gods—and as his *sukkal,* she would have access to his heavenly, numinous powers.)

Because the text is not decipherable at this point, we do not know exactly how Ninshubur defeats Enki's monsters. There is a clue, however, in Inanna's cryptic lines to Ninshubur:

Water has not touched your hand,
Water has not touched your foot.

Enki's powers are in the waters, and if water (or semen) has never touched Ninshubur, Enki can have no hold over her. Also, if water has never touched Ninshubur, she is probably pure spirit, and since she comes from the East (Ninshubur means Queen of the East), her powers, possibly connected to the sun, are able to quench those of Enki's—the water. The Queen of the East

[14]Margaret Whitney Green, *Eridu in Sumerian Literature,* Doctoral Dissertation, Department of Near Eastern Languages, University of Chicago, 1975, pp. 108–10. See this dissertation for further information on Enki.

aspect of Ninshubur is related to the cosmological Morning Star aspect of Inanna. It is Inanna's heavenly power that defeats the crafty, protean, earthy Enki.[15]

As Ninshubur overpowers each of Enki's magic creatures, the Boat of Heaven nears Uruk. There is insufficient information available to us to differentiate among the six Eridu creatures. Most likely, there is some sort of progression of power. The creatures become larger, more powerful, or more treacherous. By defeating Enki's magic creatures, Inanna acquires their corresponding shamanic powers. When she returns to Uruk, she enters as the heroic, shamanic queen. A hero wrests the treasure from the adversary; a shaman uses higher powers to protect the well-being of the community; and a queen, mother of her country, offers her people that which will nourish them both physically and spiritually.

Indeed, when Inanna returns to Uruk, she is acclaimed—and even more than she had expected. As the *me* are unloaded and presented to the people of Uruk, they are announced for the fourth time. Then, suddenly, more *me* appear than Enki had given. These *me* center on feminine attributes. At the beginning of the story, Inanna flaunted her raw feminine vitality—her wondrous vulva. En route and in battle her powers were tested, and, joining forces with more spiritual resources, Inanna emerged a fuller woman. She passed from vulva to provider, from hero to queen. Thus she was rewarded by the great Earth Shaman, Father Enki, with the "art of the woman." And this, too, she offers to the people of Uruk.

The Courtship of Inanna and Dumuzi

The brother spoke to his younger sister.
The Sun God, Utu, spoke to Inanna, saying:
"Young Lady, the flax in its fullness is lovely.
Inanna, the grain is glistening in the furrow."

It is spring when the love of the goddess Inanna and the mortal shepherd Dumuzi begins. The wheat is ripe, the lettuce is sprouting, the gardens are in bloom, water is flowing, and fresh milk is abundant. The growing, blooming aspect connects lovers and the spring earth.

In the story of "The *Huluppu*-Tree," the young woman Inanna was given a throne and bed. In the story of "Inanna and the God of Wisdom," Inanna,

---

[15]In the famous Chinese epic of *Monkey,* a similar confrontation and victory take place. The earthy, crafty magician Monkey (Enki) challenges the Great Buddha (An) but is defeated, after he hops into Buddha's hand, by experiencing the limitlessness of the heavens.

the Queen of the Land, earned her throne. Yet as "The Courtship" poems begin, the bed of the "Young Lady" is still empty.

The Sun God, Utu, who oversees and affects the growing earth, approaches Inanna and compares her sexual ripeness to the ripeness of the growing grain. By his sexually arousing dialogue with his sister, Utu takes on momentarily the role of sexual initiator, a role he refused in "The *Huluppu-Tree*," for it would have led to too close a bond between brother and sister and not have permitted the destined bond between goddess and mortal. Since Gilgamesh, the hero of Uruk, and Dumuzi were both listed as historical kings of Uruk (who ruled in approximately 2500–2275 B.C. and shared the same mother Sirtur/Ninsun),[16] they can be considered avatars or incarnations of each other. Utu incites Inanna in order to prepare her for her destiny: her marriage bed with the shepherd Dumuzi. Hence, the bond that was formed between Gilgamesh and Inanna in "The *Huluppu-*Tree" is to be consummated in "The Courtship."

But Inanna refuses. Perhaps she wishes to choose her own consort. Perhaps Inanna, who has her own garden, finds the farmer more familiar and appealing than the coarser, rougher figure of the shepherd. Dumuzi, in turn, refuses to be overlooked and offers to match his rival's gifts. Inanna protests, but Dumuzi persists, reassuring her, by comparing their families, that she and he are not so different. Yet it is only when Dumuzi fortuitously equates himself with Inanna's beloved brother Utu that he is able to spark her desire for him.

When Dumuzi actually arrives at Inanna's house bearing the gifts he had promised, Inanna runs to her mother. Surely, Ningal, "the mother who bore her," would know about love and loving. Ningal reassures Inanna by explaining that the young man will be both mother and father to her. She needn't be afraid of leaving her home, for she will find another where she will also be nourished and protected. "Open the house," Ningal advises her daughter. While Dumuzi waits, Inanna purifies and adorns herself in the hope of being admired and loved. When she opens the door of her house to Dumuzi, her outer allure delights him and his delight in her, in turn, arouses her passion. To press one's neck close to another, to put one's hand in another's, and to embrace are all Sumerian expressions for making love.

From this moment, the lovers enter their own world. Realizing her former barren state, Inanna urges the man of her heart to fertilize her—all of her. Her readiness and eagerness incite his energies, and Dumuzi blossoms. In the next several love songs, as in all deeply shared and open sexual passion, there

[16] This information is found in the historical document of the Sumerian Kinglist, which states that Dumuzi's reign of 100 years was followed by Gilgamesh's reign of 126 years. Before Dumuzi, Lugalbanda reigned over Uruk, and before him, Enmerkar built Uruk and ruled over it for 420 years.

is a mingling and intermingling of male and female energies: Inanna drinks Dumuzi's milk; he drinks hers. They dance and meet. Dumuzi offers his ripened fruit to Inanna; Inanna pours out her ripened fruit to Dumuzi. The doors to each other's houses are wide open. They call each other brother and sister, terms of affection and kinship in ancient love songs. As soul-mates, they wander together in the spring garden of life.

In the final series of love songs, Inanna calls for the royal bed her family had wished her to prepare; she sums up the love shared between herself and Dumuzi; and then commits herself to serving her king and husband in every possible way. Ninshubur restates Inanna's pledge in a more public manner: Inanna, Queen of Heaven and Earth, will serve her husband, who will be the king and servant of all Sumer and Akkad. The marriage is consummated officially and followed, almost immediately, by Dumuzi's withdrawal to kingly matters, and Inanna's bereaved memories of a lover, a brother, who was once so sweet.

The love of Inanna and Dumuzi divides into three sections. In the first section, the young woman, Inanna, still belongs to her family. Her brother guides her; her father and grandfather advise her; her mother counsels her. She is physically ready for the sexual act (the flax is in its fullness), yet she still needs time to be emotionally and psychologically prepared. The back-and-forth, pulling and tugging verbal battles so much a part of young love give the young woman and man time to try each other out and become familiar before setting sail into unknown territory.

In the second section, the lovers embark. The world of the senses so explodes about them—drinking, eating, churning, dancing, singing, tasting, smelling—that they are oblivious of everything but each other. They feed on and are nourished by one another's vital juices. The words of Inanna's mother, Ningal, are prophetic:

". . . the young man will be your father.
. . . the young man will be your mother."

In taking all their nourishment from each other, each becomes in turn parent and child, feeder and fed. Dumuzi plants the seed that nourishes Inanna; Inanna gives to Dumuzi the impulse that enables him to sprout. Yet they are more than parent and child; they are also brother and sister, equals, capable of articulating and expressing the riches that love induces. Dumuzi rejoices:

O Lady, your breast is your field . . .
Your broad field pours out plants.
Your broad field pours out grain . . .

152

Pour it out for me, Inanna.
I will drink all you offer.

Inanna sings:

My honey-man, my honey-man sweetens me always.
My lord, the honey-man of the gods;
He is the one my womb loves best.
His hand is honey; his foot is honey;
He sweetens me always.

The "always" ends. Whether by external or internal interference, unending, uninterrupted mutual bliss is not an earthly possibility. Change is the human condition. In this instance, it is the woman Inanna who by calling for the royal marriage bed brings the family and social world into her exclusive relationship with Dumuzi, thus ending "the honey-moon."

The third section reflects upon and poignantly echoes the first and second sections. The marriage bed that Inanna calls for is the very one her brother, Utu, first advised her to prepare. But now Inanna takes on the voice of *the* woman. She proclaims what she will be. What once flowed so freely and naturally between man and woman is "declared" and "determined." And then, by accepting the mandates of Ninshubur, the servant of the holy shrine of Uruk—that she will give her husband the strength to provide leadership, guidance, and fertility to others—Inanna implicitly sanctions her lover being turned into father.

As Dumuzi takes on the prescribed role of father and king, he asks Inanna to set him free; for he cannot be her exclusive paramour, making love to her "fifty times," and also serve in the manifold ways demanded of him as King of Sumer. He who once in awe and eagerness cried, "Great Lady . . . I, Dumuzi the King, will plow your vulva," now relegates the Priestess of Heaven and Earth to the role of "little daughter." He who once sought to be close to Inanna, "My sister, I would go with you to my garden," now seeks to separate himself from her:

"Set me free, my sister, set me free.
You will be a little daughter to my father.
Come, my beloved sister, I would go to the palace.
Set me free."

"The Courtship" has come full circle. Although the shepherd has become king and Inanna has found a consort for her royal marriage bed, the intimacy and passion of their "summery" love is gone. The two are together, yet separate.

These Sumerian love songs between the shepherd-king and Inanna belonged in Sumerian times to a ritual Sumerologists call the sacred marriage rite. In this ritual, the king of a Sumerian city (usually given the epithet "Dumuzi") symbolically weds the goddess Inanna, who is represented by the high priestess of her city. If the goddess is pleased with her suitor and his gifts,[17] she opens her house to him. The sacred marriage bed is prepared, and there, at the proper time (see "The Joy of Sumer" hymn and commentary), the sacred marriage between king and goddess takes place to the accompaniment of merriment and such songs as those in "The Courtship."

A detailed description of both Inanna's powers and the sacred marriage bed is given in the story of *Enmerkar and Ensuhkesdanna*. In this story, two kings of Sumer each claim to be first in Inanna's affections. The King of Aratta boasts:

> He will lie with her on the "splendid bed."
> (But) (I will lie) in sweet slumber with her on the "adorned bed."
> (He may see) Inanna at night in a dream;
> (But) (I will commune) with Inanna "face to face". . . .[18]

Then Enmerkar, King of Uruk, speaks:

> He may dwell with Inanna in the Ezagin of Aratta
> But me she will let dwell with her when . . .
>   from heaven she is standing on earth.
> He may lie with her in sweet slumber on the "adorned bed";
> (But) I on the "splendid bed" of Inanna which is strewn with pure
>   plants.
> At its back is an *ug*-lion; at its head is a *pirig*-lion:
>
> The *ug*-lion chases the *pirig*-lion;
> The *pirig*-lion chases the *ug*-lion;
> The *ug*-lion is (chasing) the *pirig*-lion;
> The *pirig*-lion is (chasing) the *ug*-lion.
>
> The day did not dawn; the night did not pass;
> I myself accompany Inanna for (15) double-hours.[19]

Inanna's powers are prodigious. She is capable of making love through the day and night. She is the cosmic force that descends from heaven to earth. Not only is she a spiritual vision in dreams, she is the awakening force that stirs love in men and ripeness in plants. No wonder kings competed for her

---

[17]An expense account recorded at the southern Sumerian city of Umma in the twelfth month around 1900 B.C. states: "one sheep and one kid [for] the wedding gifts of Dumuzi"—Thorkild Jacobsen, "Religious Drama in Ancient Mesopotamia," p. 78.

[18]Berlin, *Enmerkar and Ensuhkesdanna*, p. 43.

[19]*Ibid.*, p. 45.

favor. The man who wed such a goddess would gain fertility for himself, the farmer who wed Inanna would gain fertility for his plants; and the shepherd who wed Inanna would gain fertility for his land and people. Inanna, the Love Goddess, was "the force that through the green fuse drives the flower."[20]

In the love songs, the Sumerian farmer and shepherd compete for the affections of the Love Goddess. The Sumerian pantheon, or "family" protective of Sumer's interests, prefers the shepherd to be the one to share Inanna's marriage bed. The preference may be the result of one or several reasons: As shepherd, Dumuzi can take care of and provide for his flocks, thus proving that he can take on the leadership of the land.[21] As Dumuzi-*abzu* (*abzu* means "the deep"), the son of Enki, the God of Wisdom, Dumuzi would bring to the city of Uruk, which was previously ruled by the Sky God, An, the deep wisdom of Enki. And as a leader from the southern regions of Mesopotamia, Dumuzi would bring to northern Sumer an alliance with the more religious (and sometimes wealthier) states of southern Sumer.

The marriage of the goddess Inanna to the king was of essential importance to the people of Sumer. It was by this religious ritual that Inanna, Queen of Heaven, would take the earth-king into the "sweetness of her holy loins," and by her cosmic powers ensure the king's powers of leadership and fertility.

Yet Inanna, the Goddess of Love, does not offer her favors freely. Not only must she be properly approached with sweet words and gifts, but she must be properly and amply loved. A lion of a man is demanded: a king who is equal to Inanna in ferocity, rage, greed, power, and passion for life. And then, as the two "bed-lions"—the *ug-*lion and the *pirig-*lion—chase each other from back to front, from front to back around the bed, goddess and mortal, woman and man "chase" each other until the two become one. At that moment, at least in ritual, the bounties of heaven are assured on earth for the kingdom of Sumer—its people, its flocks, and its "holy plants."

The Descent of Inanna

FROM THE GREAT ABOVE TO THE GREAT BELOW

> From the Great Above she opened her ear to the Great Below.
> From the Great Above the goddess opened her ear to the Great
>   Below.
> From the Great Above Inanna opened her ear to the Great Below.

---

[20]Dylan Thomas, *The Collected Poems of Dylan Thomas.* New York: New Directions, 1957, p. 10.

[21]Of all ancient professions, none was more demanding than shepherding or husbandry; care and protection of animals was a twenty-four-hour-a-day occupation.

The path of the descent has "impelled" the mystic since the beginning of recorded human experience. In many traditional societies, initiatory tribal rites are often characterized by a symbolic descent into and ascent from the labyrinthian Earth Mother. These rituals give women and men the experience of being reborn on a spiritual plane. According to Mircea Eliade, traditional rituals of the descent tend to follow a universal pattern: (1) separation from the family; (2) regression to a pre-natal state, the cosmic night; (3) death, dismemberment, suffering; (4) rebirth; and (5) killing of another.[22] In other traditional societies, only certain people are "called" to travel to the underworld, for the path to the Great Below is treacherous and often there is no return. Those who do return, such as Enki, the God of Wisdom, become known as shamans and Great Magicians. They carry within them the knowledge of rebirth and often return bringing to their cultures a new world view.

Sometimes there is a specific cause that starts, or seems to start, the descent: dissatisfaction, dissolution, separation from loved ones. In modern times, Tolstoy, at the age of fifty, in good health, happily married and happily employed, wrote that there did not seem to be an apparent cause, only a "call":

I felt that something had broken within me on which my life had always rested, and that I had nothing left to hold on to, and that morally my life had stopped. An invincible force impelled me to get rid of my existence in one way or another. It cannot be said exactly that I *wished* to kill myself, for the force which drew me away from life was fuller, more powerful, more general than any mere desire. It was a force like my old aspiration to live, only it impelled me in the opposite direction. . . .[23]

Inanna is Queen of Heaven and Earth, but she does not know the underworld. Until her ear opens to the Great Below, her understanding is necessarily limited. In Sumerian, the word for ear and wisdom is the same. The ear, which is located mostly internally and is coiled like a spiral or labyrinth, takes in sounds and begins to transform the imperceptible into meaning. It is said of Enki, the God of Wisdom and the King of the Watery Deep, who lives directly above the underworld, that his ears are "wide open" and that "he knows all things." In order to fully appreciate or "know" what is said or meant, a great understanding is needed—an understanding of all things. It is the Great Below, and the knowledge of death and rebirth, life and stasis, that will make of Inanna an "Honored Counselor" and a guide to the land.

The moment Inanna opens her ear to the Great Below, her journey begins. Yet although her journey begins at once, the way to the underworld is slow and laborious. To enter the spiritual realm of the underworld, Inanna must give up her earthly powers. One by one, Inanna abandons her glory, both

[22]Mircea Eliade, *Myths, Dreams and Mysteries,* London: Harvill Press, 1960, pp. 197–200.
[23]William James, *The Varieties of Religious Experience.* New York: New American Library, 1958, p. 130.

in heaven and on earth. She abandons her seven cities and temples; she abandons her worldly strongholds:

> My Lady abandoned heaven and earth to descend to the underworld
> . . .
> She abandoned her office of Holy Priestess of Heaven to descend to
>   the underworld.
> In Uruk she abandoned her temple to descend to the underworld.

To prepare for her journey, Inanna gathers together the seven *me*. Just as a hero takes certain talismanic weapons to ensure his success, Inanna takes the seven *me*, transformed into such feminine allure as a crown, jewelry, and a gown, to serve as her protections. In case she should not return from the underworld, Inanna instructs Ninshubur in what way to remind her "fathers" of their daughter. Since Ninshubur is to enter the shrines of the gods, where their cultic images reside, Inanna's metanymic description of herself as silver, stone, and wood may refer to the materials the craftsworkers used to form the cultic statue of Inanna which, according to Sumerian belief, harbored the goddess herself. Silver, stone, and wood are also primary elements representing the three worlds: the light of heaven, the permanence of earth, and the impermanence and decay of the underworld.

At the gate of the underworld, Inanna is asked why she has come. Her first answer, "Because of my older sister, Ereshkigal," probably the true spontaneous response, expresses the compelling, not yet understandable pull of the Great Below for Inanna. Her second, more formal, ceremonial reply refers to her desire "to witness" the funeral of Gugalanna.[24] In many ways the Bull of Heaven's impetuous, forceful, procreative character resembles Inanna's. Certainly, the ever-curious Inanna would prefer "to witness" another's funeral—to gain power of and knowledge over death by proxy—rather than to experience death herself. But to enter the underworld is to see Ereshkigal, and to see the Queen of the Underworld can bring Inanna the possibility of being witness to only one funeral, her own.

Ereshkigal, the Queen of the Underworld, lives in a dry and dark realm. The *kur,* which in Sumerian also means "mountain" and "enemy territory," is the Great Unknown. Ereshkigal did not choose such a place to rule; but in "The *Huluppu-*Tree" we are told she "was given the underworld for her

---

[24]An astronomical interpretation of "the funeral of Gugalanna" (the Bull of Heaven or the planet Taurus) is suggested by the planet Taurus's yearly passage for 6 weeks below the Sumerian horizon beginning the middle of January. The re-emergence of the planet Taurus into the sky in March also corresponds to the Sumerian agricultural cycle and the yearly emergence of Dumuzi (who is often referred to as the bull) from the underworld in the early spring. See Willy Hartner, "The Earliest History of the Constellations in the Near East and the Motif of the Lion-Bull Combat," in the *Journal of Near Eastern Studies,* 12, pp. 1–16, 1965.

domain." In the underworld, she eats clay and drinks dirty water. She has no compassion for the relationships of others, husband and wife or parent and child.[25] Her one great craving is for her own sexual satisfaction. In the later Neo-Assyrian story of "Nergal and Ereshkigal," we learn that when Nergal enters the *kur,* Ereshkigal copulates with him for six days and six nights; yet when he departs on the seventh day, she still has not had enough.

Like Lilith's, Ereshkigal's sexuality is compulsive, insatiable, and without relationship or offspring. She herself bemoans her plight when she begs the gods of heaven to send Nergal back to her:

> Since I, thy daughter, was young,
> I have not known the play of maidens,
> I have not known the frolic of young girls.
> (That god whom) thou didst send and who had intercourse with me,
> Let him lie with me.[26]

This underground goddess, whose realm is dry and dark, whose husband Gugalanna is dead, who has no protective or caring mother, father, or brother (that we know of), who wears no clothes, and whose childhood is lost, can be considered the prototype of a witch—unloving, unloved, abandoned, instinctual, and full of rage, greed, and desperate loneliness.

In many ways, Ereshkigal is the other, neglected side of Inanna. Therefore, when she hears of the appearance at her gates of the "all-white" fertile, bedecked Goddess of Love, she is enraged, for Inanna's light, glory, and perpetual movement have, to some extent, been achieved at her expense. Ereshkigal commands Neti to divest the bright goddess of all she has accomplished so that the effervescent force of the universe, the ever-rising planet of the East, may experience what it is to be rejected—incapable of movement or relationship—and rendered *prima materia.*

Neti opens the gates of the underworld to Inanna. The descent, which Inanna began on earth by abandoning her seven cities and seven temples, is continued and paralleled in the underworld. At each of the seven gates (seven in Akkadian means "wholeness") Inanna is forced to give up another one of her earthly attributes. Inanna protests, yet she determinedly and heroically surrenders her roles as queen, holy priestess, and woman. Her royal power, her priestly office, her sexual powers, which had helped her in her journey and encounter with her father, Enki, are of no avail in the underworld. In fact, all that Inanna had achieved on earth weighs against her when she meets the woman at whose expense Inanna's glories had been attained. The all-seeing

[25]Alexander Heidel, *The Gilgamesh Epic.* Chicago: University of Chicago Press, 1963, pp. 122–23.
[26]Pritchard, *op. cit.,* p. 511.

158

judges of the underworld perceive Inanna's hidden, split-off parts and condemn her. Ereshkigal cries out "Guilty." And Inanna, like Gugalanna before her, is killed and becomes a part of the underworld.

The fate Inanna has chosen is the same that awaited every mortal Sumerian. However, from archaeological evidence and literary texts, it does not seem that the Sumerians believed death was the end. For them, death marked the separation of the body from the spirit. The body was buried in the ground; the spirit moved on to a different realm in the *kur*. Both at the royal cemeteries (Ur, Nippur, and Kish) and at smaller private cemeteries that have been excavated, vessels of stone and cups of lead with remnants of food and drink have been found in the hands of, or next to, the bodies of the dead.[27] In *The Epic of Gilgamesh,* Enkidu describes the vision he has had of the *kur:*

> . . . the house where none leave who have entered it. . . .
> Where dust is their fare and clay their food.
> They are clothed like birds, with wings for garments,
> And see no light, residing in darkness.
> In the House of Dust, which I entered,
> I looked at (rulers), their crowns put away;
> I (saw princes) those (born to) the crown,
> Who had ruled the land from the days of yore.
> (These doubl)es of Anu and Enlil were serving meat roasts. . . .[28]

From Enkidu's account we learn that the Sumerians believed that although no one returns from the underworld, death is not completely final. The body disintegrates, yet the transformed spirit is still recognizable. Rulers and princes become servants. Inanna, the mighty Queen of Heaven and Earth, is no longer the commanding queen; she is now at the mercy of her servant. Ninshubur, her spiritual self, must save her. Inanna can do no more.

When after three days Inanna does not return,[29] Ninshubur follows Inanna's advice and pleads before the fathers. Enlil, Inanna's father's father, the authority and director of the rational world, wants nothing to do with Inanna in the *kur*. Nanna, Inanna's father and the good son of Enlil, also has no appreciation or understanding of why Inanna might have gone on such a journey. Both Enlil and Nanna are angry that Inanna should pursue a direction that is different from theirs. But Enki, Inanna's *mother's* father and the God

---

[27]Woolley, C. Leonard, *Excavations at Ur,* Ernest Benn, Ltd, London, M54, p. 145.
[28]Pritchard, *op. cit.,* p. 87.
[29]The three-day period may be connected to the moon's disappearance from view for three days each month. This relates to Inanna's aspect as First Daughter of the Moon. (We do not have sufficient information at present to correlate Inanna's Venus aspect—Lady of the Morning and Lady of the Evening—with astronomical fact.)

of Wisdom, has compassion for his daughter who is in difficulty. Not only does the God of Wisdom value the journey she has set out upon, but he does not forget his daughter's significance. Inanna is Queen of Heaven and Earth; her existence is vital to all the lands.

As God of Wisdom, Enki has powers to create and to facilitate. He knows the nature of the feminine *kur,* and of its rule by the jealous, anguished Ereshkigal, who at this moment is moaning "with the cries of a woman about to give birth." He creates from the dirt of his fingernails the *kurgarra* and *galatur*—instinctual, asexual creatures who will not disturb the necessary infertility rules of the *kur.* He endows the creatures with the artistic and empathetic talent of being professional mourners, capable of mirroring the lonely queen's emotions.

At the same time that Ereshkigal is moaning both for her "inside" and her "outside," Inanna is dying. Ereshkigal had willed Inanna's death; yet she can scarcely bear it, for Inanna is the other side of herself. The interplay between Inanna and Ereshkigal is complex and dynamic. Although Inanna had seemed to descend without cause to the *kur,* it might now be understood that Ereshkigal, or the dark side of Inanna, had gone into labor and needed to be reborn. It was this labor or "call" that Inanna had heard from the Great Above.

Ereshkigal, the neglected side of Inanna, has certain qualities that are similar to Lilith's. Both are connected to the nighttime aspects of the feminine —the powerful, raging sexuality and the deep wounds accumulated from life's rejections—which seek solace in physical union only. Lilith usually flees from rejections; Ereshkigal withdraws "underground." In "The *Huluppu-*Tree," when Lilith could not have her own way, she resentfully and destructively smashed her own home. The powerful Lilith of Inanna's adolescent days had to be sent away so Inanna's life-exploring talents could be developed. But now that Inanna has become queen of her city, wife to her beloved, mother to her children, she is more able to face what she has neglected and feared: the instinctual, wounded, frightened parts of herself. She now hears, and is capable of responding to, the labor call of Ereshkigal in the Great Below.

When Ereshkigal moans, the *kurgarra* and *galatur* moan with her. The anguish she feels in the deep underworld is appeased by the echo of their concern. Ereshkigal is so touched by the attention they offer to her in her pain that she extends herself and offers, in turn, gifts of fertility and growth. But the creatures, following Enki's instructions, refuse these gifts and ask her instead for what she wishes to give and yet for that which is most difficult for her to give. They ask her to release part of her personal anguish, her despair and anger, which is embodied in the glorious Goddess of Love. Yet by having permitted herself to be comforted and to experience the pleasure of the rapport with the other, Ereshkigal has already released part of her pain. Her agreement to release her nemesis, Inanna, is only the confirmation of the spiritual movement that the God of Wisdom and Healing, Enki, had understood and had most ingeniously brought about.[30]

The triad—Ninshubur, Inanna's spiritual self; Enki, the God of Wisdom and Healing; and the compassionate, instinctual *kurgarra* and *galatur*—is successful.

Once reborn, Inanna wishes immediately to leave. However, in the Sumerian underworld, while a record of each arrival is kept, no one had ever before been allowed to depart. But Inanna's case is different. She has been reborn in the underworld. Therefore new rules must be introduced. With the proclamation of the gods of the underworld:

No one ascends from the underworld unmarked.
If Inanna wishes to return,
She must provide someone in her place . . .

the rules of the underworld are both stretched and maintained. Inanna may leave, but she is responsible for finding someone to replace her.

A part of Inanna must return. A passageway has been created from the Great Above, the conscious, to the Great Below, the unconscious, and it must be kept open. Inanna must not forget her neglected, abandoned older "sister" —that part of herself that is Ereshkigal.

Inanna leaves the underworld, accompanied by the *galla.* In their uncompromising aspect of refusing all gifts, the *galla,* or demons of the underworld, are the living representations of the *kur:* death accepts no deals, physical, emotional, or familial. Moreover, the *galla* have the additional, riveting aspect of belonging to the one for whom they are intended.

Meanwhile, Inanna's servant and two sons,[31] who care deeply about her, have abandoned the routine of their daily lives. Ninshubur waits by the gate of the underworld for Inanna. Shara and Lulal, Inanna's sons, wait for their mother in their temples, most likely praying. All three have taken off their customary clothes and put on sackcloth, the garment of mourning.

Yet the King of Sumer goes on with life as if nothing had happened, as if the Queen of Heaven and Earth had not disappeared, as if his own wife were safe and secure. Near the apple tree where he and Inanna had once made love, Dumuzi, dressed in the noble *me-* garments his wife had given him, seated on

---

[30]See Sylvia Perrea's *Descent to the Goddess* (New York: Inner City Books, 1981) for a further exploration of the healing aspects of "The Descent of Inanna."

[31]Our only information about Inanna's two sons, according to Samuel Noah Kramer, comes from two sources. In "Enmerkar and the Lord of Aratta," Shara proclaims: "I am a wild beast . . . a warrior . . . a noble lord . . . the son of Inanna and the god of the king." In a composition that seems to be a lamentation, Inanna gives birth to Lulal, the water scorpion, the water snake, whose cry is the cry of the Flood.

the royal throne, which his wife, Inanna, had also presented to him, clings to his new role of kingship and refuses to acknowledge the ties of feeling and love that once bound him to his wife.

When Inanna's inner ear opened and she departed from Uruk, she was in midlife, married, with two children. Through her instructions to Ninshubur, Inanna made careful provisions so that she would return. However, during her absence Dumuzi had been following a completely different journey. Inanna had turned from earthly passion and achievement to the Unknown; Dumuzi had turned from earthly passion to earthly achievement. Once shepherd, now king, kingship has become his path. He has grown so attached to and identified with his high position that he neither weeps for his "lost" wife nor runs to greet her when she returns, as do her sons and Ninshubur.

The impasse between Inanna and Dumuzi at this moment is reflected in their physical positions. The Queen of Heaven, tormented by underworld-demons, stands below her husband. Dumuzi is raised above the earth and maintains his high seat and glorious, shining garments. To understand this crucial and brutal encounter, it is worth hypothesizing on both of their thoughts:

Dumuzi: I ruled the kingdom, kept order while she adventured into chaos. Now she wants to reclaim her authority on earth. Her unsettling journey and demons bring turmoil into the kingdom. They are her concern, not mine. I must continue to carry out my all-consuming task of governing the people and state of Sumer.

Inanna: I placed him on the throne, gave him his position. I loved him and he left me to attend to affairs of state. While I went to deal with matters affecting my deepest soul, he used my powers to make himself more important. Once I was his whole world; now he refuses to descend from his throne to help me.

Whatever may have been the specific personal grievances between husband and wife that allow us to identify with the story, the greater issue is already determined. Someone must go to the underworld to replace Inanna. And the husband of Inanna is the perfect substitute, for he is also the King of Sumer.

The Sumerians extolled the king who was wise and compassionate as well as powerful. They extolled the king who cared for the weak, the poor, the wronged, the widowed.[32] It was Inanna's visit to the underworld that opened the Queen of Heaven's vision to her own vulnerability. If Dumuzi is to be a

[32]The plaque of Ur-Nammu (see page 9 for illustration) states that the king was responsible for ensuring that the orphan did not fall a prey to the wealthy, that the widow did not fall a prey to the powerful, that the man of one shekel did not fall a prey to the man of one mina [sixty shekels]"—Kramer's essay, page 118.

truly "great" king in the ways extolled by the poets of Sumer, he too must journey to the feared place, to the Great Unknown. He, too, must meet Ereshkigal. Inanna's curse topples Dumuzi from his fixed position and forces him to face the dark, demanding aspects of his wife, as well as the uncontrollable, inexplicable, irrational mystery of death and the kingdom of Ereshkigal.

Filled with terror, Dumuzi resists the *galla* who seize him. Yet as Inanna's husband, as well as Dumuzi-*abzu*, the son of the God of Wisdom, he has the inner capacity to undergo such a journey. Just as Inanna needed time to descend, abandoning one city and temple after another, Dumuzi, too, in fleeing from Uruk to Kubiresh to Old Belili, prepares himself to leave the earth for his own journey of transformation.

THE DREAM OF DUMUZI

> His heart was filled with tears.
> The shepherd's heart was filled with tears.
> Dumuzi's heart was filled with tears.

As "The Dream of Dumuzi" begins, the heart of the shepherd-king is filled with tears. The ruling king who once sat so proudly on his noble throne, permitting himself little compassion toward others, now is overwhelmed by his own feelings and vulnerability.

He leaves the city to return to his boyhood home of the steppes. There he calls on the familiar natural forces—plants and animals—to comfort him. He calls to his mother and sister; he has lost his strength and vitality and can no longer provide for them. Alone, without power, comfort, or direction, he turns inward and dreams.

Nightly dreams are usually of a daily, mundane character. Once a year, or perhaps only once in a lifetime, we dream a "Great Dream." We sense its overwhelming importance. The Great Dream speaks of more than the here and now; its images are riveting. It will not give us peace until we begin to understand it.

In ancient literature, Great Dreams often emerge at moments of intense confusion or turmoil; and the one who can interpret the dream and find direction for the dreamer then becomes invaluable to the dreamer. At the end of *The Odyssey,* Penelope speaks of the dreams from the Gate of Ivory that are illusions, and the dreams from the Gate of Horn that, when understood, accurately describe the future. The constant Penelope tells her dream to the disguised wanderer Odysseus. He not only interprets it but helps to bring it to pass. In the Bible, the powerful Egyptian Pharaoh frees the lowly Hebrew slave, Joseph, from prison so that Pharaoh can profit from Joseph's wisdom. Once Joseph interprets Pharaoh's dream, the fate of the two—ruler and slave,

Egyptian and Hebrew—becomes linked. It often takes a person of opposite character from the dreamer to interpret the dream, for the dream speaks of the inner life that lies hidden away from its dreamer.

Until now, all that Dumuzi had needed to rule his kingdom—sceptre, crown, measuring rod and line, fields, meadows, and forests—had been given to him. Understanding, compassion, devotion belonged to others. But now, it is these very qualities that Dumuzi needs. Therefore, he turns to the feminine wisdom of his younger sister. The compassionate Geshtinanna explains his dream image by image. The message of the dream is devastating: for Dumuzi there is no escape from the forces that will carry him to his death. Yet, buried within the dream, there is a small detail portending life and hope.

Dumuzi's dream divides into five sections. In the first section, the larger natural world, symbolized by the rushes, reeds, and trees, turns against him. In the second section, the tools of Dumuzi's profession and manhood—his hearth, churn, drinking cup, and shepherd's crook—are taken away and destroyed. In the third section, Dumuzi's life instinct—the lamb and the sparrow —has been crushed. Dumuzi is no longer welcome on earth. He has lost his livelihood. His feet cannot move, nor can his spirit (in the form of the sparrow) ascend. All that is left to him is the mourning and grief of his sister. Just as Ninshubur, *at Inanna's request,* wept for Inanna and saved her life, so it is Geshtinanna who is to take up Dumuzi's spirit and not let it die.

In the fourth section, the memory of Dumuzi is safeguarded in the immortal aspect of Geshtinanna's animals. The one detail portending hope for Dumuzi is the *lapis* beards of Geshtinanna's goats. Just as the grief of the animals for their lost shepherd is to be permanent, so too the sister's grief is to go beyond the momentary; Geshtinanna, in her enduring vigil, will save Dumuzi's life.

In the fifth section, shepherd and man are destroyed, returning Dumuzi's kingdom to the primordial forces. Although the kings of Sumer continuously battle to conquer the wilderness and secure their cities and sheepfolds from flood, famine, and enemies, the devastating power of "the winds" is ever-present, ever-threatening. (In Sumerian, the word for wind, *lil,* also means "ghost" and "demon.")

Despite Geshtinanna's realization of the inescapable devastating power of the demons, when the *galla* appear, she urges Dumuzi to hide. The *galla* search for Dumuzi. For material profit, Dumuzi's friend betrays him. Dumuzi then curses his friend's child. However, it was not so long ago that Dumuzi had considered the *me-* garment and his high throne more valuable than his ties to his wife. It is the compassionate Geshtinanna who puts an end to the perpetuation of rejections and curses, pain and anger. Dumuzi turns to his sister, and she bravely and adamantly befriends him.

The *galla* continue to pursue Dumuzi. Dumuzi appeals to Utu, and pleads his case by reminding Utu of their shared family ties:

> O Utu, you are my brother-in-law,
> I am the husband of your sister.

Utu, the God of Justice, remembers the shepherd, whom he had first suggested that his sister marry. He enables Dumuzi to assume the forms of the slow, lowly snake and the swift high-climbing mountain gazelle. By taking on the skin of different animals, Dumuzi is given the opportunity to experience the varying forms of his earthly kingdom. But the *galla,* who belong to Dumuzi, discover him in each disguise.

Resigned, Dumuzi returns for the last time to the sheepfold and his sister. The sheepfold or "womb" is the Great Earth Mother, who gives birth and takes back the dead. Much as Inanna had been forced to do when entering the underworld, Dumuzi, too, is divested of his kingship, his shepherdship, his achievements, and his virility. The most imperceptible of things, Dumuzi's dream, has now come to pass.

THE RETURN

> "You will go to the underworld
> Half the year.
> Your sister, since she has asked,
> Will go the other half.
> On the day you are called,
> That day you will be taken.
> On the day Geshtinanna is called,
> That day you will be set free."

Inanna, Sirtur, and Geshtinanna weep for the departed Dumuzi. They weep for their husband, son, and brother. The depth of Geshtinanna's grief leads her to offer her life to share her brother's death. Her offer is of such magnitude that the mind can scarcely grasp its meaning. The instinct to live, to survive, becomes secondary. Love transcends life.

After losing her bridegroom through her uncontrollable willfulness, Inanna realizes she has lost the "sweetness" of life. In "The *Huluppu-*Tree," the young Inanna wept because she could not get her way. In "Inanna and the God of Wisdom" and "The Courtship," she was able to channel her resources to achieve her desires. But now, having returned from the underworld charged with her own dark, ruthless powers, the widowed Inanna grieves because she has pushed her way through and destroyed the bridegroom and husband she loves.

When the bereft and humbled Inanna meets Dumuzi's sister, Geshtinanna's words pierce her heart:

"I would find my brother! I would comfort him!
I would share his fate!"

Once Inanna was also Dumuzi's "sister." They nourished and comforted each
other; they delighted in each other; they shared each other's days and nights.
When Inanna and Geshtinanna meet on the streets of Uruk, the two sides of
the feminine—passion and compassion, willfulness and feeling—meet. But
mourning and suffering have subdued Inanna's raging passion; and Geshtinanna's words awaken her nurturing, compassionate side.

Throughout the Cycle of Inanna there has been an intense relationship
between the heavenly sister and brother, Inanna and Utu, as well as between
the earthly sister and brother, Geshtinanna and Dumuzi. Both brothers acted
as sexual initiators and protectors for their sisters;[33] both sisters relied upon
and supported their brothers. In heaven, the sky gods, Utu and Inanna, com-
plement each other; Utu, the Sun God, rules the sky by day, Inanna, the
Morning Star and Evening Star (known to us as the planet Venus), rules the
sky at dawn and twilight. On earth, Dumuzi and Geshtinanna share the yearly
planting cycle.

The sister-brother couples are first drawn together in "The *Huluppu-*
Tree" when Inanna asks the earth hero, Gilgamesh, to help her. Later, in "The
Courtship," it is Utu who suggests Dumuzi as a fitting consort for his heavenly
sister. Surprisingly, it is the sky gods Inanna and Utu who initiate the relationship with their earthly counterparts.

After the marriage of Inanna and Dumuzi, there is a reversal of roles. The
immortal Queen of Heaven *descends* into the earth and dies; while the mortal
Dumuzi *ascends* his throne, striving, much like a sky deity, for greater power
and glory. This reversal is then turned about when Inanna condemns Dumuzi
to enter the underworld. Because of this reversal, the humbled earthly brother
and sister seek help from the sky deities. Dumuzi appeals to Utu to save him
from the demons and Geshtinanna appeals to Inanna to find her brother. The
cross-tie of marriage between Inanna and Dumuzi provides the link that opens
up new relationships between brother and brother and sister and sister.

Geshtinanna's transcendent words of compassion stir Inanna from her
state of isolation and self-pity. Just as her older widowed sister, Ereshkigal, had
been moved by the compassionate words of her healers; so, too, the widowed
Inanna is touched by the warmth of her earthly sister. And she, too, grants her
healer a boon: she releases Dumuzi from her angry curse and allows Gesh-

---

[33]In *The Sacred Marriage Rite,* Kramer includes a poem in which Dumuzi initiates his sister
in the sheepfold, p. 103.

tinanna to share his fate. The favors are returned from the sky deities to their earthly sister and brother.

In her youth, Inanna's contact with her earthly brother, Gilgamesh, propelled her into life, activity, and achievement. Later, her journey to the underworld connected her with the buried, rejected parts of herself. Now it is the presence of her earthly sister, Geshtinanna, that completes Inanna's journey on earth. Through Geshtinanna, Inanna is reconnected to Dumuzi, to an *other,* and so to all of life.

The two "sisters" are led by the "holy" fly to the lost brother. The bloodless fly, that part of nature so seemingly without import or substance, is yet alive and, like all of life, craves a fate and meaning. It demands a boon from Inanna. In response, Inanna draws into her story those who also seek meaning: the people of Sumer. Inanna grants the fly permanent residence in the taverns and access to the culture of Sumer, which, most likely, flows with the beer and wine. As a result of Inanna's boon, the high talk of the wise ones is to be accompanied by the tiny buzzing of the lowliest of living creatures—a constant remainder that it was the lowliest of creatures who, by its connection to the realms of death, was able to reunite their king and goddess.

At Arali, a stopping place on the way to the Great Below, Inanna takes Dumuzi's hand and blesses Dumuzi and Geshtinanna with both eternal life and death. The loving sister is given her request: she will comfort her brother and share his fate. But she will not be able to unite with her brother on earth. Dumuzi is to remain Inanna's husband. The once seemingly surprising and yet vital relationship between sky goddess and earthly hero can now be more fully understood. The union of opposite realms—that of the fixed, willful, judgmental aspects of the sky deities with the ever-changing, emotional aspects of earthly mortals—brings about greater personal integration for individuals as well as greater prosperity and fertility for the gods and the community of Sumer.

Half the year the goddess Inanna and the king Dumuzi will be united; and half the year they will be separated. For half the year, Dumuzi will actively rule over Sumer. He will join Inanna on the sacred marriage bed, a ritual all Sumer will join in celebrating (see Hymn Seven). The milk will flow in the sheepfold, the wheat will ripen, the apple trees will blossom. But then, as the seasons change and the harvest passes, Dumuzi will enter a period of inactivity, quietude, and meditation. He will surrender his worldly powers, constructs, and conventions. He will become a part of the stasis—of that which ineluctably "is." He will return to Ereshkigal.

> The force that through the green fuse drives the flower
> Drives my green age; that blasts the roots of trees
> Is my destroyer.[34]

[34]Dylan Thomas, *op. cit.,* p. 10.

The choice of a period of six months as the time of separation is probably related to the concomitant agricultural cycle, in which Geshtinanna, "root-stock of the grapevine,"[35] reigns over the wine whose grapes and figs are harvested from the Sumerian earth each autumn: while Dumuzi, in his aspect of Damu, the power in the growing grain, reigns over the beer, whose barley grows in the earth the other six months of the year, to be harvested in the spring.

Paradoxically, although Dumuzi seems to be separated from Inanna six months of the year, he is actually wed to her all year, for in the winter as he rests with Ereshkigal, he is staying with the dark, instinctual side of Inanna. Since Dumuzi is married to the composite goddess Inanna-Ereshkigal, he is to experience all of the woman. Not only is he to "know" the love goddess, he is to "know" the Goddess of Death as well. To live with the light side of the goddess half the year and the dark side the other half would seem to require superhuman powers; and indeed, when the king Dumuzi weds Inanna, the title of deity is affixed to his name. With Inanna's proclamation, Dumuzi's marriage takes on a sacrificial nature. But as the spiritual king of his people, this is justified. Dumuzi, King of Sumer, is to live in a perpetual state of initiation. The spiritual awakening of man, according to Inanna's proclamation, is to be required of the king.

At this moment at the end of the story, when Inanna acts as divine ordainer, she shifts from active participant in her life story to constellated divinity. She who opened up for the first time the passage between the conscious and the unconscious now retreats, giving over the task to the more human participators, Dumuzi and Geshtinanna. They are now responsible for keeping open the passage from the Great Above to the Great Below.

Inanna's journey to the underworld has brought a new world order to Sumer. The ramifications of her proclamation are manifold. By giving Dumuzi eternal life half the year, Inanna changes the cosmic pattern. Love, which parallels the normal course of the human life cycle—budding, blooming, and dying—is henceforth guaranteed, by being linked to the seasons, an annual renewal. The king who enters the underworld once a year will emerge every six months renewed in feminine wisdom and inner strength to take over the leadership and vitality of the nation. Moreover, by alternating the descent between sister and brother, feminine and masculine, the women and men of Sumer (at least in ritual) share in the necessary journey into and out of the mountain.

Inanna's establishing of the annual ritual of descent and ascent offers a model of parity to the female-male relationship. Acknowledging the duality of life dying into death and death leading into life gives the participants in the

[35]Jacobsen, *Treasures of Darkness*, pp. 62–3.

168

ritual the opportunity of annually renewing their relationships to the cosmos, to each other, and to their goddess.

But none must forget that the wisdom of Inanna's decree and its manifold ramifications have been attained for all of Sumer by Inanna's response to, journey toward, and encounter with the fierce, forbidding, and terrifying queen, Ereshkigal—Inanna's other self. "For whoever has not known himself has known nothing, but whoever has known himself has simultaneously achieved knowledge about the depths of all things."[36]

> Holy Ereshkigal! Great is your renown!
> Holy Ereshkigal! I sing your praises!

Seven Hymns to Inanna

In the beginning of time, the universe was divided into three realms: heaven, earth, and the underworld. Inanna's journey through these realms as related in "The Descent" describes a soul's ripenings. When she returns from her journeys below to her place of origin in heaven, she is a completed soul and, as such, Inanna comes into her divinity.

The hymns to Inanna acknowledge her myriad achievements and aspects. She is radiant, thundering, destructive, defiant, judgmental, kind, generous, peaceful, healing, erotic, decisive, discerning, wise, transcendent, loving, fertile, joyous, and ever youthful. Parts of Inanna's characteristics can be seen to have emerged from her encounters with the bold, decisive hero Gilgamesh, the wise, form-making Enki, the fertile, erotic, eager young shepherd Dumuzi, the powerful, authoritative King Dumuzi, the just, all-seeing Utu, as well as with the "fixed," judgmental Ereshkigal and the generous, compassionate Geshtinanna. But the fullness of Inanna's being goes beyond these separate aspects. Inanna is the Goddess of Love. Formed from all of life, the Goddess of Love gives forth desire that generates the energy of the universe.

The seven hymns, known as the Iddin-Dagan Hymns, included in this cycle are attempts by the Sumerian temple poet to reveal Inanna's glory and to come close to, as well as to attract, the Goddess of Love, so that she will descend once again from heaven to earth. The first six hymns may have been recited on varying occasions. W. W. Hallo writes that the hymns to Sumerian deities and kings may have been created for dedications of new temples or statues or at festivals involving public processions of statues.[37] The seventh

---

[36]Elaine Pagels, *The Gnostic Gospels,* New York City: Random House, 1979, p. 19.

[37]W. W. Hallo, "The Cultic Setting of Sumerian Poetry," *Actes de la XVII Rencontre Assyriologique Internationale,* Comité Belge de Recherches en Mesopotamie, Ham-sur-Heure, Belgium, 1970, pp. 116–34.

hymn clearly was recited in celebration of King Iddin-Dagan's divine union with the goddess Inanna. Although the names of specific instruments do not introduce the different hymns in this composition, string instruments and drums such as are noted in the third and seventh hymns often accompany the recitation. It seems likely that the antiphon or refrain that occurs in the last four hymns of this composition would have been accompanied by one or several instruments.

1. THE HOLY PRIESTESS OF HEAVEN

The first hymn to Inanna is a greeting. Her radiance and light are welcomed from afar. As the daughter of the Moon God, Nanna, she belongs to the sky deities, who are worshipped for their awesome power, consciousness, majesty, and transcendence.

2. LOUD THUNDERING STORM

By means of a monthly ritual, the second hymn to Inanna changes the perspective of the worshipper from that of a distant bystander to that of a "captured" participant.

In the first twelve lines, all that is mysterious, awesome, and beyond human control or knowledge—both in the external world of the raging storm and in the internal world of the emotions of the heart—is likened to the persona of Inanna.

Unfortunately, the fifty lines that connect the passionate, destructive, troubled Inanna to the composed, magnanimous, and all-knowing Inanna are not decipherable. When the text begins again fifty lines later, "the crescent moon reaches its fullness." The implicit comparison between the wild, terrifying Inanna and the dark of the moon suggests that they were both accepted and viewed by the Sumerians as mysterious, awesome, and uncontrollable parts of life. Yet both in heaven and on earth, dark and frightening moments are followed by calm and order: the moon in the heavens grows, lessens, disappears, but then takes its form on the seventh day of each month; the earthly woman, who often experiences a disequilibrium at the start of her menstrual period, finishes the disorder of her cycle on the seventh day of the month. By joining the menstrual cycle to the moon's cycle in a monthly ritual, the wild, frightening, and disorderly parts of life are subsumed into a predictable and reassuring order.

Thus the moment each month when the crescent moon took its shape was a time of great import for Sumer, for it symbolized the time when the raging Inanna purified herself and assumed her role as *divine woman,* wife to Dumuzi, the King of Sumer, and guide to her people. It meant that the inchoate time of chaos and instinct had ended, and that form was to be reestablished.

Once Inanna takes up the *me*, the holy form of things, she assumes her destined role, and her spiritual force moves from the wild and unpredictable "heart" to the all-knowing and all-seeing "eye." So, too, the animals, people, and gods who are governed by their uncontrollable instincts go before their queen in order to discover their own form and destiny. What they discover is the experience of being linked to the "eye" or inner light of their goddess. The incredible energy of the storming goddess, now brought into the social order, emanates with such luminosity and intensity that the people are captured and lifted into a state of "greater light." This spiritual impulse is given grounding in the many forms of expression (from specific vocations to such abstract pursuits as "truth" or "the art of kindness") offered in the holy *me*.

3. THE HOLY ONE

The third hymn releases the worshipper from a state of "captivity" to a more equitable relationship with the goddess. With a devotional ceremony or parade, the people of Sumer honor their goddess. They praise her with music and dress; by initiatory sacrifice, they both release and rejoin themselves to her "light."

In the parade, the women and men wear androgynous clothing, symbolic of the Goddess of Love, who exists as the opposite sex in each person. By adorning one side of themselves with the clothing of the opposite sex, both women and men "create" themselves in the image of their goddess. The various activities—both sexes eagerly entering the moving circle of the jump ropes, the men singers carrying the feminine hoop, and the cultic group of female priests, carrying the masculine double-edged ax and sword—all exemplify the desire of experiencing the fullness of the self.

As the colorful procession nears Inanna, who most likely is seated in the form of the high priestess at the top of the temple steps, one priest destroys the wholeness of life by offering blood before the holy priestess. One can imagine that as the blood is given the pulsating beat of the music suddenly stops in anticipation. But it begins again almost immediately with the tinkling tambourine. The ecstatic sacrifice, expressing the offer of the population to give their life to their goddess, who gives them life, has been accepted.

This seemingly miraculous appearance of Inanna in her heavenly aspect is most likely timed to the appearance of the Evening Star in the darkness. Inanna's heavenly manifestation, akin to the rainbow in the sky after a storm, marks the goddess's promise to Sumer to guide and watch over her people as a divine shepherdess would watch over her sheep. From this moment of exchange between mortal and goddess, the refrain—"My Lady looks in sweet wonder from heaven"—begins and continues throughout the hymns in this cycle. The refrain heralds the bond forged between the goddess and her people, which by the act of sacrifice and its acceptance has become a physical blood tie as well as an abstract visual one.

4. THE LADY OF THE EVENING

5. THE LADY OF THE MORNING

6. THE LADY WHO ASCENDS INTO THE HEAVENS

The next three hymns celebrate the daily relationship between the Queen of Heaven and her followers. In Hymns Four and Five, Inanna, the Lady of the Evening and the Lady of the Morning, is a manifestation of a stable, dependable cosmic order that divides, organizes, and guides life's activities. Twice daily Inanna gives to her followers what is appropriate.

At twilight, the Lady of the Evening's radiant light guides the people and creatures of Sumer to their place of rest and love. The westerly sunset images of Hymn Four center on the feminine Inanna: night, animals, gardens, reeds, food, rest, lovemaking. At dawn, the Lady of the Morning's clarity of light reveals and settles the proper judgments in society, so that the people of Sumer can direct their energies toward their day's work. The sunrise images of Hymn Five are grouped around the masculine Inanna: dawn, judgment, thought, action, abstractions. Together, Hymns Four and Five create a dependable order, a personalized deity, composed of clearly feminine and masculine characteristics.

Another side of Inanna is the Lady Who Ascends into the Heavens. The Inanna of Hymn Six is feared by her people. This Inanna belongs to the emerging-dissolving epiphany of existence, the awesome miracle of rebirth, for she appears when the sky is empty and dark. In the moment of terror between day and night, when there is *nothing,* when all seems lost and void, then Inanna, the first one to brave the empty skies, appears.

In return for Inanna's different manifestations of light, the people offer her appropriate gifts. For her guidance by day and night, they kneel before her, singing her praise and offering her cooked food. For her miraculous presence, they bring Inanna the scent of life—incense—as well as the signs of divine life—every kind of raw and cooked food.

The people who parade before the three Inannas sing her praises, for they yearn to fulfill their own feminine and masculine natures, as well as to come close to the Goddess of Love, the transcendent force of life, which permeates all of existence. And Inanna, confirming her continuing relationship with the people of Sumer, partakes of their gifts and appears to them morning and evening on the horizon, the meeting place of heaven and earth:

My Lady looks in sweet wonder from heaven.
The people of Sumer parade before the holy Inanna.

172

Inanna, the Lady Who Ascends into the Heavens, is radiant.
I sing your praises, holy Inanna.
The Lady Who Ascends into the Heavens is radiant on the horizon.

7. THE JOY OF SUMER

Hymn Seven is the culmination of the seasonal, monthly, and daily ties created between Inanna and Sumer. In Hymn One, Inanna, solitary and separate, is greeted from a great distance. In Hymn Two, the people of Sumer are raised into a relationship with their goddess, a relationship which, in Hymn Three, is formed by their act of sacrifice and its acceptance. By Hymns Four, Five, and Six, Inanna is in constant relationship with her people. And in Hymn Seven, she descends from heaven to enter into direct union with the people of Sumer through their earthly king, Dumuzi.

Inanna's descent is needed to set in motion the annual cycle of life on earth. According to the *me,* which dictate the order and form of things, a New Year's Day is ordained that marks the earth's awakening to new life. All year the people have brought their goddess tribute in the form of plants and animals, her creations. But now, when the earth is ready to be seeded, to bring forth plants which will give the people the holy power of life, and when the new moon has just been reborn, the divine spark is needed once again. The mystery of human life, connected to the mystery of natural life, dwells with the Goddess of Love. It is she who brings fertility to all things. The sacred bed, strewn with her holy plants and designed with her symbol of the lion, is thus carefully prepared to entice the Queen of Heaven to earth.

After making love, both Inanna and Dumuzi shine with inner joy. Inanna's cosmic light, which shines from the heavens all year, this day appears on earth. The king invites the people to join in their happiness. The king, queen, musicians, and people celebrate with feasting and singing. The magic moment is upon them: male and female, heaven and earth, mortal and divine have united and a new year has begun. The spirit of love has descended and is reborn on earth. The king acknowledges the source of the people's and the gods' delight:

Mighty, majestic, radiant, and ever youthful—
To you, Inanna, I sing!

ANNOTATIONS
OF THE ART

by Elizabeth Williams-Forte

Inanna's City: Uruk

Inanna's city, Uruk—modern Warka—lies 150 miles (250 km.) southeast of Baghdad and 12 miles (20 km.) from the Euphrates, a branch of which skirted the ancient city known in the Bible as Erech. Systematic excavations have been conducted at Uruk for over fifty years by a German archaeological expedition and have uncovered levels of occupation dating from the fourth through the first millennium B.C. By far the most important for our knowledge of the goddess Inanna and of ancient Sumerian civilization, however, are the levels dating to c. 3500–2900 B.C. These levels (VI–III) provide evidence of the earliest known urban civilization, characterized by the first truly monumental temple architecture and art and by the first writing.

A complex, class-stratified society must have administered the building of these architectural complexes and imported the materials, such as stone and metal, that were not available locally but were transformed by specialized craftsmen into cult statues and vessels, tools and weapons. Although the processes that led to the transition to urban life in Mesopotamia are believed to have begun several centuries prior to the so-called Uruk period, the appearance of the hallmarks of civilization at Uruk is sudden and evokes the story of the *me* that Inanna took from Enki and Eridu to bring back to her people in Uruk.

The sacred place of Inanna, the Queen of Heaven, is called Eanna, the "House of Heaven," and is the oldest preserved temple on the site of Uruk. In level V–IVb at Uruk appears a complex of enormous temples that exhibit the characteristic features of all later Mesopotamian temple architecture: mud-brick construction with elaborate niche decoration, a three-part plan composed of two aisles flanking a nave, and at the end of the nave, the "Holy of Holies." The largest of these temples, over 30 by 80 meters in size, possesses a limestone base—an unusual and lavish feature in a region where mud bricks are the common building material and stone is rare.

A smaller shrine of mud brick lies at a right angle to and across a court from the "Limestone Temple." Covering the mud-brick walls of the court is a distinctive mosaic-like decoration formed of individual baked clay cones. The heads of the clay cones are dipped in red, black, and yellowish-white paint, then thrust into the mud substructure of the wall to create textile-like geometric patterns. Above the court and adjacent to the temples stands a hall composed of two rows of the earliest examples of free-standing columns, each over 2 meters in diameter and also decorated with the colorful clay cones.

Within these temple complexes and the successive temples built on the same holy ground over a period of several centuries were found the first cylinder seals and clay tablets bearing the first writing, characteristic features of Mesopotamian civilization until the first millennium B.C. Cylinder seals—small tubes of stone with designs carved upon their cylindrical surface—were rolled in wet clay used to seal storage jars and to make clay tablets. Numerous cylinder seal impressions on pieces of clay used to seal vessels were found in the Limestone Temple and nearby buildings. Two methods were employed to secure these vessels: wet clay was either packed into the mouth of the vessel or it was pressed over a knotted string used to secure a piece of cloth or leather that covered the jar. The cylinder seal was then handrolled in several directions over the clay to form unbroken friezelike designs that served with the clay plug to secure the jar's contents.

In a slightly later level at Uruk were found clay tablets bearing seal impressions, numerals, and then the first writing, pictographic in form. These very first written documents were tallies and records of the administration of the temple, which served as the center of Sumerian economic, industrial, and religious life. Writing probably developed as a means to keep track of the economic activities of the temple, providing documents of the number of sheep, the amount of barley, and the like that were brought to the temple by the farmers and shepherds, then redistributed to them and the remainder of the populace of Uruk by the temple managers.

Cylinder seals also may have served an economic function. For the surface designs of the cylinder seals produced complex non-duplicatable impressions on the clay jar sealings and tablets, showing animals, mythological creatures, and ritual scenes involved with the cult of Inanna. The seal-impressed clay thus provided the temple officials with a sure means of determining if temple goods had been tampered with, and may also have served to identify the vessels' contents or owners. The impression of a seal on a table probably legitimized the transaction recorded there either in numerals or pictographic script by the temple official who witnessed the transaction in the name of the goddess. Indeed, if only indirectly, the symbols of Inanna must have alluded to the goddess as the ultimate source of all the goods and thus of the economic activities of the temple, and must also have provided a potent apotropaic, protective function for both the tablets and temple goods on which they appeared.

The ritual significance of the seals is evidenced by the scenes engraved upon them, showing Inanna's gatepost and rosette symbols and perhaps Inanna herself in human form (page 27), her temple, and her sacred flocks and herds (page v). Other impressions depict the "man in the net skirt," probably the *en* or lord of Uruk (page 85). This figure's responsibilities as the priest who assumes the role of the goddess's consort and as the king who becomes the temporary war leader are portrayed: he performs sacred rites before Inanna's temple (page 106) and views prisoners or slaves bound hand and foot before him. Vases and sculpture in relief and in the round found at Uruk were probably also central to the cult of the goddess. The vases embellished with relief sculpture and stone inlay in rosette form must have been for use in the temple.

The most important vessel, known as the "Warka Vase," was carved with three registers of relief, the top showing Inanna in human form, or perhaps her priestess, before her temple receiving offerings brought by the *en* of Uruk (page 104). The riches of the land are brought to the goddess on this vessel, just as they may have been deposited before her image in the sanctuary of her temple. Fragmentary remains of enormous cult images of the goddess may have been found at Uruk in the form of two stone sculptures of female faces. These imposing visages, one of alabaster, the other of gypsum, may have been joined to bodies of some perishable material like wood and embellished with precious metals and fine garments.

Thus the inhabitants of ancient Uruk provided their patron goddess, Inanna, whom they envisioned in human form, with all the necessities of their own lives but on a grander scale. For her they built a "House of Heaven"— enriched by bright colors, adorned with sculpture, and laden with vessels filled with produce recorded in detail by the temple scribes—in gratitude for the gifts of civilization, the *me,* which Inanna had brought to them from Eridu and which the excavations have revealed within her sacred city, Uruk.

I would like to thank Dominique Collon of the British Museum and François Tallon of the Louvre for their help in expediting the photographs of the illustrations.

With only a few exceptions, the ancient artifacts chosen to illustrate the stories and hymns of Inanna derive from the region and general era in which these myths originate—that is, ancient Mesopotamia during the late fourth through early second millennium B.C. Certain photographs show only a detail or a motif excerpted from a larger work of art in order to more clearly elucidate the relationship between image and text. The use of such details is noted in the documentary information that precedes each commentary. Specific details regarding place and date of origin, dimensions, and other information have been included in the art commentaries when available. Full bibliographic citations for sources mentioned in the commentaries can be found in the Selected Bibliography.

ii   *Inanna with Date Palm*
Fragment of a relief vessel inscribed to Entemena of Lagash. Mesopotamia. Early Dynastic period, c. 2400 B.C. Basalt. Berlin, Staatliche Museen

An enthroned goddess gazes benignly out at the viewer from this fragment of relief from a vessel inscribed to King Entemena of Lagash. On her head is a horned crown flanked by feathers. On top of the crown is a small frontal face. Heavy masses of hair fall around the goddess's face and over her shoulders, ending in spiral curls. She grasps a date cluster, and stalks surmounted by blossom-like forms grow from her shoulders. These attributes suggest that she is a vegetation goddess.

Her frontal visage and the dates she holds might suggest that she is Inanna as the goddess of the date storehouse, her original title and significance according to Thorkild Jacobsen. If so, perhaps the blossoms are the rosettes of Inanna, and the small face, bird feathers, and talons on her crown those of *Anzu*, the lion-headed thunder-bird that Jacobsen maintains is also her emblem. The *Anzu*-bird that made its home in the summit of the *huluppu*-tree to Inanna's dismay, and that coveted the *me* eventually won by Inanna, may appear here as the tamed opponent now an embellishment of her holy crown.

v   *Sheepfold with Sheep and Gateposts of Inanna*
Trough. Mesopotamia. Jemdet Nasr period, c. 3000 B.C. Limestone. 1.3 m. London, The British Museum. Photograph courtesy of Hirmer Verlag, Munich.

Lambs issue from either side of a sheepfold bearing the doorpost symbols of Inanna, marking these sheep as the property of the god-

177

dess and her temple. The sheep that crawl from Inanna's sheepfold (a pictographic sign that also represents the vulva) are always young animals and thus may be symbolically "born" from the womb of this goddess of fertility.

The *Hullupu*-Tree

3   *Woman, Goddess, and Date Palm*
      Cylinder seal (impression). Mesopotamia. Akkad period, c. 2330–2150 B.C. Green schist. London, The British Museum, BM 892360

A date palm is flanked by two seated figures wearing long garments. To the left appears a female figure, with her hair held up by a headband. Her mirror image, the figure opposite her, is identified as a deity by its horned crown. Each figure gestures (with upturned palm) toward the tree between them. From beneath the throne of the divine being writhes an upright serpent.

Although the *buluppu*-tree may have been a willow, the most frequently represented tree in Mesopotamian art is the date palm. The date palm was an important economic source for the ancient Mesopotamians. Its fruit is of great nutritional value and can be preserved and stored; its leaves, fiber, and timber provide numerous by-products; and it survives easily in the salty soil and water of Mesopotamia. These factors, together with the fact that the date palm requires the services of a horticulturalist in pollination if a substantial crop of dates is to be harvested, must explain its frequent appearance in Mesopotamian texts and art.

Inanna herself, according to Thorkild Jacobsen, is called "Lady of the Date Clusters" and represents the numen of the communal storehouse for the dates. Her spouse, Dumuzi, called *Amaushum-galanna,* "The one great source of the date clusters," is personified in the enormous bud that the date palm sprouts each year—the source of the leaves, flowers, and fruit. In Sumerian art, the date palm stands before deities and is the focus of libations and, perhaps, symbolic ritual fertilizations (see page 9).

5   *Planting a Tree*
      Relief vessel. North Syria, Mari. Early Dynastic period, c. 2500 B.C. Steatite. h. 20 cm. Damascus Museum. Photograph taken from André Parrot, *Sumer,* pl. 169.

On this vessel fragment a kneeling male figure and a horned animal flank a hatched panel that probably represents the trunk of a palm tree. At the base of the tree, which seems to separate the cultivated garden from the wilderness, appear two saplings. The sapling to the right is possibly being planted by the male figure. The animal seems to prepare to trample or perhaps graze upon the second sprout. In the field around the animal to the right appear other perhaps herbivorous creatures. To the left an undulating serpent rises as if to strike at the underbelly of the kneeling man. Framing this scene is a wavy band and a guilloche, which may symbolize the water that nurtures the vegetal and animal life that appears above.

Such vessels formed of easily carvable stone, such as steatite or chlorite, are found at third millennium B.C. sites stretching from eastern Iran to the Gulf and throughout Mesopotamia to the north Syrian site of Mari, where this fragment was found.

6   *Lilith*
Clay plaque. Mesopotamia. Isin-Larsa–Old Babylonian period, c. 2000–1600 B.C. Baked clay. Paris, Louvre, AO 6501

A nude, winged, bird-footed goddess wears a crown composed of multiple horns. Her gaze directly engages the attention of the viewer as she stands frontally, with both hands uplifted, palms facing outward. Beneath her taloned feet appear two horned animals back to back.

A demonic composite being, part-bird, part-human, is represented on this clay plaque. Her delicately modeled nude body is juxtaposed with powerfully clawed bird feet and wings that fall behind her like an open veil. She has been identified as the dark maid Lilith, called "screech owl" in a biblical passage (Isaiah XXIV:14). Like that nocturnal bird, Lilith makes her home in the trunk of a tree, the *huluppu-*tree of Inanna.

7   *Snake with Interlacing Coil*
Cylinder seal. Ur, Mesopotamia. The Royal Cemetery, Early Dynastic period, c. 2600–2500 B.C. Lapis lazuli. Iraq Museum. Photograph courtesy of the British Museum, U1 9080.

The majority of the pictorial surface is covered with the intertwined coils of a serpent, forming a lattice pattern. To the right its tail appears below the coils and its head above, with a bird perched upon it.

Two snakes intertwined rather than one are shown on earlier representations of this motif. Snakes twist themselves together in this fashion when mating, suggesting this symbol's association with fertility.

The close relationship between snakes and tree roots has been pointed out by Thorkild Jacobsen, especially in connection with the chthonic god Ningishzida, "Lord of the Good Tree," whose symbol is the serpent. The underground source of the tree's life, its roots, become the writhing serpent emblem of the anthropomorphic god. On this seal, the entwined serpent perhaps represents the subterranean sphere in which the tree's winding roots exist and to which the snake returns to hibernate, just as the snake made its home in the roots of the *huluppu-*tree.

8   *Anzu-Bird*
Relief plaque of Dudu (detail). Tello (Girsu), Mesopotamia. Early Dynastic period, c. 2450 B.C. Bituminous stone. Paris, Louvre. Photograph taken from W. Orthmann, ed., *Der Alte Orient,* pl. 88.

This eagle is the embodiment of the thundercloud, floating as a cloud on its outstretched wings, its lion head emitting a roar like thunder.

9   *Enthroned Goddess, God, and Date Palms*
Stele of Ur-Nammu. Ur, Mesopotamia. (Two details from stele are set facing each other.) Third Dynasty of Ur, c. 2050–1950 B.C. Limestone. Philadelphia, the University Museum, University of Pennsylvania Photograph taken from André Parrot, *Sumer,* pls. 282–283.

King Ur-Nammu, identified by the inscription on this stele, pours a libation over a date palm planted in a vessel placed before a goddess on the left, and repeats the libation before a god on the right of this relief. Each deity wears the multiple-horned miter and flounced robe characteristic of divinity and sits upon a throne in the form of a temple. The goddess gestures toward the king with upraised hand, while the god extends the "rod and ring" toward the libating figure.

King Ur-Nammu, the founder of a dynasty that initiated a revival of traditional Sumerian culture in southern Mesopotamia, is shown on this relief (one of five, each 3 meters high), performing his pious duties to the god and goddess of Ur: Nanna, the Moon God, and his spouse, Ningal. The king's role as "gardener" responsible for nurturing vegetation by his union with the goddess may be symbolized by this action.

The rod and ring extended to Ur-Nammu by the god have been interpreted as a measuring rod and line, to be used in laying out the plan of Nanna's temple, for the building of the Moon God's shrine is portrayed on another register of this relief. These implements may also be emblems of kingship, like the *pukku* and the *mikku* fashioned by Inanna for Gilgamesh.

Inanna and the God of Wisdom

11   *Flowing Vases*
      Fragment of relief. Tello (Girsu), Mesopotamia. Gudea period, c. 2144–2124 D.C. Limestone. h. 15.5 cm ; w. 11. 7 cm. Paris, Louvre. Photograph taken from André Parrot, Sumer, pl. 243.

      On this fragment of relief "flowing vases" appear. Two streams of water gush from each vase to intermingle with those issuing from its neighbor. The flowing vase is the symbol of Enki and also of abundance, like the cornucopia. The two streams may represent the two major rivers of Mesopotamia, the Euphrates and the Tigris. A Sumerian text discussed by Samuel Noah Kramer relates that the Tigris was formed by the semen of Enki.

13   *Enki in the Abzu receiving Isimud*
      Cylinder seal. Mesopotamia. Akkad period, c. 2330–2150 B.C. Black serpentine. 30 × 19 cm. New York, Pierpont Morgan Library, Corpus 202

      The god Enki holds his emblem, the vase from which flow two streams of water. The corners of his sacred chamber are embellished by spiraling volutes, perhaps evoking the watery nature of the *Abzu* where Enki made his home. Before the God of Wisdom stands his minister, Isimud, whose two faces look in opposite directions. The doorposts grasped by two nude heroes frame the scene and designate the entrance to the *Abzu*. As an acolyte of the Water God, Enki, the nude hero frequently holds a flowing vase or, as here, a doorpost. The association of the doorpost with Enki may allude to his role as the patron of foundations.

181

14, 15 *Banquet*

Cylinder seal (upper and lower impression). Ur, Mesopotamia. The Royal Cemetery, c. 2500 B.C. Lapis lazuli. 48 × 25 mm. London, The British Museum, U 10939

Lifting their cups to each other, a ritually bald male figure sits opposite a female figure. Servants stand before and behind the enthroned banqueters, whose importance is indicated by their size.

As related in this text, journeys of the gods to holy cities to visit relatives or patrons frequently culminated in banquets. Whether the banquets represented here depict such a divine symposium is difficult to determine because none of the participants wear the emblem of divinity, the horned crown. However, this seal was inscribed to a Queen of Ur, Pu-abi (Shubad), within whose grave it was found. Thus the banquet shown here may depict some type of annual festival in which the queen or a priestess participated, perhaps in the guise of a goddess.

16–18 *Cuneiform Writing*

Samuel Noah Kramer has transcribed in his own writing the cuneiform for the specific *me* given in each of the first lines of the fourteen groupings of the *me*.

19 *Crescent-Shaped Boat*

Cylinder seal. Mesopotamia. Neo-Sumerian period, c. 2112–2004 B.C. Steatite, h. 16 mm.; d. 7 mm. Brooklyn, New York, The Brooklyn Museum, L 71.21.10

A flat-bottomed boat with inward-curving prow and stern floats upon zigzag lines, probably symbolic of flowing water. The round form with netlike markings that surmounts the boat may be a canopy or hut for either passengers or storage. Reeds indicative of the marsh-like environment along the rivers in southern Mesopotamia flank the boat.

21 *Seven-Headed Monster*

Cylinder seal (detail of impression). Tell Asmar, Mesopotamia. Akkad period, c. 2350–2150 B.C. Gray stone. 3.2 × 2.2 cm. Iraq Museum.

Seven snake heads with forked tongues characterize this dragon-like creature. Four of its heads have been slain and hang limply.

22 *Giant Monster*
Cylinder seal (detail of impression). Khafaje, Mesopotamia. Early Dynastic II, c. 2750–2600 B.C. Shell. 2.8 × 1.8 cm. Iraq Museum. Photograph taken from André Parrot, *Sumer,* pl. 201.

This demonic hybrid creature is formed of human, leonine, and serpentine characteristics. It has a frontal masklike face and human torso. The lower body is composed of two lions whose tails have serpent heads that bite at the creature's head and are grasped by its human arms.

23 *Running Monster*
Cylinder seal (detail of impression). Mesopotamia. Early Dynastic II, c. 2750–2600 B.C. Onyx marble. 3.7 × 2.4 cm. New York, Pierpont Morgan Library, Corpus 61. Photograph taken from André Parrot, *Sumer,* pl. 169.

A kneeling composite creature, with one leg uplifted as if running, is shown on this seal. Its spiky arms terminate in lion heads, while its head is formed of a single large eye surmounted by two hornlike projections.

25 *Reed Boat Approaches City Shrine*
Cylinder seal (left side). Tell Billa, Mesopotamia. Late Uruk–Jemdet Nasr period, c. 3200–3000 B.C. Black diorite. h. 4.3 cm; d. 3.5 cm. Iraq Museum, IM 11953. Photograph courtesy of Corethia Qualls.

A reed boat is directed, punted, and paddled to a temple by three bald, ritually nude male figures. On the shore, a shrine façade stands between two pillars composed of reed bundles topped by three pairs of rings. These "ring-bundles" may be the emblem of a male god, perhaps Dumuzi, based on their appearance elsewhere on cattle byres (another symbol of that deity), just as the doorpost with streamer emblem of Inanna appears above sheepfolds.

26 *Gift Bearers*
Cylinder seal (right side). Tell Billa, Mesopotamia. Late Uruk–Jemdet Nasr period, c. 3200–3000 B.C. Black diorite. h. 4.3 cm; d. 3.5 cm. Iraq Museum, IM 11953. Photograph courtesy of Corethia Qualls.

Gifts associated with the goddess and with the figure in the net skirt, probably her consort, appear in the hands of offering bearers to the right. The first carries a long, beaded belt or necklace; the second has hands clasped in prayer; and the third carries the long belt worn by the net-skirted figure in other scenes.

27   *City Shrine Surrounded by Signs of Inanna: The Rosettes, her Face, and Her Gate-posts.*
       Cylinder seal. Tell Agrab, Mesopotamia. Jemdet Nasr period, c. 3000 B.C. White limestone. h. 5 cm.; w. 4.4 cm. Iraq Museum. Photograph courtesy of the British Museum.

The surface of the seal is divided horizontally by an arched line. Beneath it appears a temple, flanked by two gateposts. Evenly spaced above the temple in the upper register are two eight-petaled rosettes, the flower or star symbol of the goddess Inanna. Above the arch, where its two ends meet in a V-shaped, chinlike form, is a face. The face is dominated by an enormous pair of oval eyes above a round nose and oval mouth. Similar enormous oval eyes in association with rosettes appear on a vessel excavated at Uruk in the sacred precinct of Inanna—Eanna, the House of Heaven.

The Courtship of Inanna and Dumuzi

29   *Man and Woman*
       Clay plaque. Diqdiqqah near Ur (U 17604), Mesopotamia. Isin-Larsa–Old Babylonian period, c. 2000–1600 B.C. Baked clay. London, The British Museum, BM 123230

A god and goddess stand facing frontally with arms around each other's waist. Each wears a horned crown, the emblem of divinity, and a flounced robe that leaves one shoulder bare. Their faces are carefully modeled and their expressions dignified. The goddess's hair is held up in a chignon, while the god's falls into heavy curls alongside his long beard.

Between two trees growing from mountain-like forms appear two horned animals, one above the other in the field. The animal on top rests, with its legs tucked beneath its body; below, the second creature appears to kneel, perhaps to drink from a brook indicated by the slightly undulating line beneath its snout.

30 *Wheat and Sun Symbols*
Fragmentary back of a chariot. Larsa, Mesopotamia. Isin-Larsa–Old Babylonian period, c. 2000–1600 B.C. Baked clay. 7.1 × 6 cm. Paris, Louvre, AO 16959

This fragmentary terracotta plaque shows three standards surmounted by orbs, the upper parts of which are missing, with a central drilling. Such orb standards are often interpreted as solar emblems, symbolic of the Sun God, Utu. Between the standards appear two long-necked birds before two stalks of vegetation.

32 *Man with Wheat*
Cylinder seal (detail of impression). Mesopotamia. Late Uruk–Jemdet Nasr period, c. 3200–3000 B.C. White limestone. h. 6.2 cm.; d. 4.3 cm. Paris, Louvre, AO 6620

A man in a short net skirt holds two stalks of grain.

35 *Shepherd Herding His Sheep*
Cylinder seal (lower half). Mesopotamia. Uruk period, c. 3400–3200 B.C. Yellow limestone. h. 5.7 cm.; d. 5 cm. Berlin, Staatliche Museen, VA 7234

To the rear of a herd of long-eared sheep their shepherd appears with his staff and a flail.

36 *Inanna with Staff*
Clay plaque. Mesopotamia. Isin-Larsa–Old Babylonian period, c. 2000–1600 B.C. Baked clay. 11.9 × 6.6 cm. Paris, Louvre, AO 12456

Inanna stands in full regalia on this terracotta plaque. Her crown is adorned with multiple horns of divinity, her body with the divine garment of flounced material. Around her neck she wears multiple-beaded necklaces. In her outstretched hand she holds the emblem composed of a mace flanked by heads of lions, her sacred animal.

Baked clay plaques like this were made from molds and were thus infinitely reproducible. Such plaques bearing images of deities may have been private devotional images, for they have been found in the excavation of private houses at Mesopotamian sites.

38   *Water and Vegetal Design*
Cylinder seal. Mesopotamia. Early Dynastic period, c. 2800 B.C.
Shell. h. 3 cm.; d. 1.8 cm. Berlin, Staatliche Museen, VA 510

Undulating lines suggestive of water or vegetation cross the
seal's surface diagonally. From each side of these diagonal motifs
sprout small, branchlike lines. Near them are randomly placed oval
forms.

40   *Goddess and Tree Spirit*
Cylinder seal (detail of impression). Tello (Girsu), Mesopotamia.
Akkad period, c. 2330–2150 B.C. Serpentine, h. 3.5 cm.; d. 2.2 cm.
Paris, Louvre.

Beneath a tree is sheltered a kneeling goddess with her arms
outstretched to receive a god whose upper body emerges from the
base of the tree. Both deities wear miters with multiple horns indicative of their high rank, and the god extends a mace, an emblem of
gods and kings, to the goddess.
The deities on this seal are probably embodiments of natural
forces. The falling tree with its crown touching the ground may be
dying from the heat of the sun. The god rising from the trunk of the
dying tree would then symbolize the rebirth of vegetation, as suggested by Pierre Amiet.
On this seal, the poses and gestures of the anthropomorphic gods
are strikingly similar to Inanna and Dumuzi's actions in this passage
of "The Courtship": the goddess kneels with arms outstretched to
receive the god, who rises like a sprout from the tree before her. In
"The Courtship," Dumuzi rises up from fallen leaves to consummate
his marriage with the goddess, thus producing new vegetation that
pours forth from Inanna's womb. The dying of the tree in the fall and
its rebirth in the spring seem to be enacted here—just as in "The
Courtship of Inanna and Dumuzi"—by divine beings whose love for
each other perpetuates fertility in the world and ensures the seasonal
cycle.

41   *Star-Shaped Rosettes*
Cylinder seal. Mesopotamia. Jemdet Nasr period, c. 3000 B.C. Chal-
cedony. h. 4.2 cm.; d. 1.5 cm. Berlin, Staatliche Museen, VA 2031

A dense pattern of geometric forms covers the field of this seal.
Enormous four-pointed rosette-like stars dominate the design. Sur-

rounding them are "Maltese crosses" and circles with central drillings.

This four-pointed star may be associated with Inanna, for it is similar to the eight-pointed rosette-star that appears as her emblem. That Inanna already in the earliest periods was considered the goddess of the planet Venus is confirmed by an inscribed clay tablet from Uruk, level IIIb. On the tablet appear the pictographs for "festival," "star," "Inanna," "day," and "to set." Adam Falkenstein interprets these signs to mean the festival on the day on which the star of Inanna sets.

The remaining motifs may also have had a religious or protective significance for the owner of the seal.

43   *Lovers Embracing on Bed*
Clay plaque. Mesopotamia. Isin-Larsa–Old Babylonian period, c. 2000–1600 B.C. Baked clay. Basel, Erlenmeyer Collection.

Short, horizontal strokes score the edge of a bed upon which lie embracing male and female figures. The bearded man cups his partner's head in the palm of one hand and rests his other hand upon her waist. The long-haired woman, her neck adorned by multiple necklaces, encircles her companion's waist with one arm, offers him her breast with the other, and places her foot upon his.

Such scenes are considered representations of the cult of the sacred marriage, which took place annually in each Mesopotamian city. The union of the city's patron god or goddess and their divine consort ensured the prosperity of all living things in the coming year. The actual participants in the ritual were the king of the city and the high priestess of the temple. It is they who may be portrayed on this small clay model of a bed.

The purpose of small clay plaques such as this is not certain. The religious scenes they bear may have served an amuletic purpose for the owner, providing specific magical benefits such as the protection or blessing of certain divine beings.

Numerous lead plaques of couples making love, as well as lead and clay plaques of scorpions, were found deposited in the vicinity of a late second millennium B.C. temple to Inanna/Ishtar at Ashur in northern Mesopotamia. It has been suggested that such plaques were brought by worshippers as offerings to the temple and in some cases taken away as tokens of worship offered there.

Inanna's Gateposts
Detail of the upper register of the "Warka Vase." Uruk (level III),
c. 3100–2900 B.C. Alabaster. h. 3 ft. Iraq Museum. Photograph courtesy of Hirmer Verlag, Munich.

These polelike objects are the gatepost emblems of Inanna and
appear as her symbol in both the art and the earliest pictographic
script from her city, Uruk. They most frequently appear as a pair and
are thought to designate the entrance to her temple. These emblems
are probably composed of a bundle of reeds tied with bands. Some
houses in modern Iraq are still constructed of such reed bundles. On
the basis of the ring and streamer at its summit, this emblem's architectural function has been suggested to be that of a doorpost. A
pole passing through the rings would support a mat that was lowered
to close the door, and raised and secured (perhaps by the streamer)
to allow worshippers to enter the temple.

The role of the doorpost as a kind of "sentry" guarding the
vulnerable entrance to the temple rendered it an important apotropaic, protective emblem in later art. Certainly, this tall emblem
with its long streamer surmounted by a round ring is evocative of the
female form, and is perhaps a sort of "totem" of the goddess Inanna,
as suggested by Adam Falkenstein.

49   *Votive Statue of King*
Statue of King Lamgi-Mari. Mari, North Syria. Early Dynastic period,
c. 2500 B.C. White stone. h. 27.2 cm. Aleppo Museum. Photograph
taken from W. Orthmann, ed., *Der Alte Orient*, pl. 30.

Lamgi-Mari, King of Mari, stands facing us with one bare foot
slightly advanced. Both hands are held at waist level, one grasping the
wrist of the other. His hair is worn parted and gathered in an elaborate chignon, the characteristic hairstyle of kings in the late Early
Dynastic period (c. 2600–2400 B.C.) in Mesopotamia. The priest-
kings of the religious hierarchy that controlled the city-state in the late
fourth millennium B.C. gradually evolved into the kings of the third
millennium B.C., who lived in palaces, served as war leaders, and
assumed some priestly responsibilities.

This statue of King Lamgi-Mari bears a dedicatory inscription on
the shoulder not covered by the elaborate flounced robe. The inscription states that this is a votive statue, dedicated to Inanna/Ishtar,
within whose temple at Mari the statue was found. Votive statues like

this were surrogates for their owners, placed in the temple to offer continuous prayers to the deity.

The Descent of Inanna
From the Great Above to the Great Below

51   *Goddess from the Other World*
     Cylinder seal. Isin-Larsa–Old Babylonian period, Mesopotamia. c. 2000–1600 B.C. Hematite.

An enormous winged bird-footed goddess stands frontally with hands clasped. A double register scene appears alongside her. In the upper register a nude goddess and a bearded deity receive homage from human worshippers. A row of composite beings appear in the lower register. A fly, a hedgehog (?), and a human head appear above these creatures in the field.

This goddess with bird features has been identified with Lilith (see page 6). She may represent the chthonic aspect of Inanna/Ishtar derived from her association with the demonic and frequently bird-like creatures and gods that inhabit the underworld. Here, the goddess's horned head appears alongside deities and their human worshippers while her bird-feet appear beside demonic creatures. The hierarchical arrangement of this scene may signify her dual nature, partially of "heaven and earth" and partially of the underworld.

52   *Inanna on Her Throne*
     Cylinder seal. Mesopotamia. Akkad period, c. 2330–2150 B.C. Nephrite. 4.3 cm. Private collection. Photograph taken from W. Orthmann, ed., *Der Alte Orient,* pl. 135H

During the period of Akkadian control of Mesopotamia (c. 2334–2154 B.C.), the early Sumerian "Lady of Heaven" and fertility goddess Inanna merged with the Semitic Ishtar, a warrior goddess. The goddess Inanna/Ishtar appears on this Akkadian seal, seated on a throne decorated with two crossed lions. Weapons, including a scimitar and a mace, rise from her shoulders as she gestures to two worshippers and looks full-face at the viewer. Her flounced garment covers only one shoulder, and her long hair falls in curls down to her elbows. To the left of Inanna/Ishtar stands an attendant goddess wearing a single-horned miter. To her right a female figure gestures in worship and pours a libation into a vessel.

55 *Door to the Underworld*
Clay plaque. Mesopotamia. Isin-Larsa–Old Babylonian period, 2000–1600 B.C. Baked clay. h. 6 × 5 cm. Paris, Louvre AO 9007

An open door leads into the interior of a rectangular terracotta box that probably represents a shrine. Inside sits a bird-beaked figure, wearing the long flounced robe characteristic of divinities.

57 *Goddess in Underworld*
Cylinder seal. Mesopotamia. Akkad period, c. 2330–2150 B.C. Hematite. h. 3.5 cm.; d. 2.2 cm. Paris, The Louvre, AO 2485

Flanked by two forms shaped like mountains, perhaps symbolic of the *kur* (the underworld), stands a frontal-facing goddess. Undulating rays or flames rise from her shoulders and may indicate either her solar or infernal nature. A ring—possibly similar to the ring that was taken from Inanna when she entered the fifth gate of the underworld —is held in her hand.
To the right, within one mountain, a deity with rays or flames rising from his shoulders grasps the tail of a bull-man. To the left, a deity with a scourge stands grasping the horn of another deity who collapses within another flaming mountain. A small figure kneels beside the mountain to the left.

60 *Scorpions and Rosette*
Stamp seal. North Mesopotamia. Gawra period, c. 3300 B.C. Steatite. h. 14 mm (base to apex); w. of base: 33 mm; 1.41 mm. Brooklyn, New York, The Brooklyn Museum, L. 71.11.2

Inanna's symbol, the eight-pointed star or rosette, appears between the pincers of two scorpions on the square face of this stamp seal.

61 *Goddess Entreating*
Cylinder seal (detail of impression). Mesopotamia. Akkad period, c. 2330–2150 B.C. Marble. h. 3.6 cm.; d. 2.6 cm. Paris, Louvre. (Image repeated on following pages.)

Many Mesopotamian prayers had to be spoken out loud and accompanied by specific gestures. According to Leo Oppenheim, the best attested of these prayers is the type named *šu·ila,* or "uplifted hands."

On this seal, a goddess stands with an uplifted hand, perhaps performing a similar prayer-like ritual. Uplifted hands are characteristic of goddesses in Mesopotamian art, especially during the Neo-Sumerian and Old Babylonian period, c. 2100–1600 B.C. Such goddesses have been identified as *lama,* female protective beings that Oppenheim calls "angels." These goddesses served as supplicants on behalf of human worshippers, offering prayers for their well-being.

63   *Goddess Pleading Before Enki*
Cylinder seal. Mesopotamia. Akkad period, c. 2330–2150 B.C. Marble. h. 3.6 cm.; d. 2.6 cm. Paris, The Louvre

A supplicating goddess of lower rank, indicated by her single-horned miter, approaches the enthroned Enki flanked by his two-faced minister Isimud and his acolyte, the nude hero. With her arm uplifted and her hand held before her mouth, she appears as a supplicant to Enki.

72   *Attacking Demons*
Cylinder seal. Ischali, in the Diyala region, Mesopotamia. Isin-Larsa–Old Babylonian period, c. 2000–1600 B.C. Hematite. h. 2 cm; d. 1 cm. Courtesy of the Oriental Institute, University of Chicago, A 17004 (Ish. 34:129)

A kneeling figure with upraised arm is attacked by demonic creatures with leonine heads and bird feet, and by a male figure with multiple mace and scimitar.

The exact nature of the demonic figures is difficult to determine, but the association of birdlike beings with the nether world is common in the Near East and the Aegean. The *galla* are described as those "who flutter over heaven and earth" in "Dumuzi's Dream" (see page 79), suggesting their birdlike nature. And as Henri Frankfort has shown, soul-birds in Egypt and harpies and sirens in the Aegean area all objectified certain aspects of terror inspired by death. The frightening, bird-clawed monsters with gaping mouths may represent similar underworld beings threatening the small cringing man with death.

191

74 *Cattle Byres*
Cylinder seal. Late Uruk–Jemdet Nasr period, c. 3200–3000 B.C.
Magnesite. h. 5.3 cm.; d. 4.8 cm. Oxford, Ashmolean Museum, 1964,
744

In the lower field of this seal appear three reed cattle byres. Each
byre is surmounted by three reed pillars topped by rings, a motif that
has been suggested as symbolizing a male god, perhaps Dumuzi.
Within the huts calves or vessels appear alternately; from the sides
come calves that drink out of a vessel between them. Above each pair
of animals another small calf appears. A herd of enormous cattle
moves in the upper field.

82 *Leaping Stag*
Cylinder seal. Middle Assyrian period, c. 1300–1200 B.C. Milky chal-
cedony. h. 3 cm.; d. 1 cm. New York, Pierpont Morgan Library,
Corpus 601

A stag leaps with upflung leg through a wooded, mountainous
region, indicated by the twisted trees and scale pattern representing
the mountain from which it grows. A small bird is perched on a
thistle-like plant beneath the tree.

The Return

85 *King Feeding Rosette Flowers to Sheep*
Cylinder seal. Mesopotamia. Late Uruk-Jemdet Nasr period, c. 3200–
3000 B.C. Marble. h. 5.4 cm.; d. 4.5 cm. Berlin, Staatliche Museen,
VA 10537

A bearded male figure wears a round cap and a skirt with netlike
pattern. This man appears on many artifacts excavated at Inanna's city,
Uruk, and may represent the *en,* or priest-king, of that city, who
assumes the role of divine consort of Inanna in the sacred marriage
ceremony. Clasped to his chest are two curving branches ending in
rosette-flowers. These rosette symbols of Inanna are nibbled by

maned sheep, literally portraying the nourishment of the flocks ensured by the union of the goddess and her consort. The emblems of Inanna that flank the scene suggest that it is taking place within the sacred precinct of her temple.

89   *Dying Man*
Cylinder seal. Mesopotamia. Neo-Assyrian period, ninth century B.C. Serpentine. 42 × 19 mm. Toronto, Canada, Lands of the Bible Archaeology Foundation, Royal Ontario Museum

A sick or dying man lies beneath a reed hut. Attendant figures, perhaps exorcist priests, lean above him and kneel at the head of his bed. Sacred dogs of Gula, the Goddess of Healing, leap about the exterior of the hut.

Seven Hymns to Inanna

91   *Stars*
Cylinder seal. Mesopotamia. Early Dynastic I, c. 2900–2750 B.C. London, The British Museum, BM 119304

An enormous four-lobed, starlike rosette dominates the pictorial field on this seal. It is surrounded by smaller rosette-stars, dotted circles, and triangles.

1. The Holy Priestess of Heaven

92   *Radiant Inanna*
Cylinder seal. Mesopotamia. Akkad period, c. 2334–2154 B.C. Black stone. h. 4 cm.; d. 2 cm. Courtesy of the Oriental Institute, University of Chicago, A 27903

Inanna/Ishtar in full regalia stands triumphantly with one foot upon the back of her roaring lion. Her head is crowned by a headdress of multiple horns. Weapons issue from her shoulders, while enormous wings appear from behind her back, suggesting both her martial and supernatural nature. In the sky beside her appears her eight-pointed star, emblematic of her manifestation as the Venus star. Another goddess wears a single-horned miter, denoting her lower rank, and gestures in worship to the Queen of Heaven and Earth.

94   *Rain Goddess*
Cylinder seal. Mesopotamia. Akkad period, c. 2334–2154 B.C. Shell.
33.5 × 19.5 mm. New York, Pierpont Morgan Library, Corpus 220

Inanna/Ishtar may appear on this seal in her manifestation as
Rain or Thunderstorm Goddess, as suggested by Elizabeth Douglas
Van Buren. Nude except for her horned crown, she stands between
the wings of a lion-bird or griffin, probably a manifestation of the
embodiment of the thunder-bird, *Anzu*. Streams of rain are held by
the goddess and vomited by the lion-bird as it draws the chariot of
the Weather God, who snaps his lightning whip. The clatter of the
wooden wheels may be accompanied by the roar of the lion-bird as
thunder. This scene gives mythopoeic form to the visual phenomena
of rain, lightning, and thunder—its aural accompaniment in nature.

96   *Woman and Man; Crescent, Star, and Bird*
Clay plaque. Diqdiqqah, near Ur., Mesopotamia. Neo-Sumerian pe-
riod (Ur III), c. 2000 B.C. Baked clay. London, The British Museum,
BM 127473 (U 18496)

This baked clay plaque, found in a grave in the Diqdiqqah cemetery near Ur, shows a man and a woman facing each other. The
woman reaches out to rest her hand on the man's shoulder, while he
places his hand on her waist. Each wears a full, rounded coiffure and
elaborate garment. The female figure has multiple necklaces and a
flounced garment. The long beard of the male—rendered by a series
of short incisions in the clay—reaches to the border of his garment,
which crosses his body diagonally, freeing one shoulder. Below the
couple's arms is a bird; above, a moon crescent surmounted by a star.

96   *Eye*
Cylinder seal. Mesopotamia. Early Dynastic period, c. 2800 B.C. London, The British Museum, BM 128839

An abstract design formed of parallel curving lines creates an
eyelike effect on the surface of this cylinder seal.

98   *Parade*
Cylinder seal. Tell Asmar, in the Diyala region (As 32.120), Mesopotamia. Akkad period, c. 2334–2154 B.C. Carnelian. h. 3.9 cm; d. 0.8
cm. Courtesy of the Oriental Institute, University of Chicago,
A 11367

In this seal's upper-left register, a deity, perhaps Inanna/Ishtar,
stands upon a lion and gestures in greeting to two worshippers. The
first worshipper gestures toward the goddess; the second figure, perhaps nude, clasps its hands before its chest. Behind the goddess appears another deity, wearing a multiple-horned miter and holding a
mace across its shoulder. A bare-headed figure with clasped hands
stands to the right. In the lower register appears a procession of five
worshippers identical to this bare-headed figure.

4. The Lady of the Evening

100   *Goddess standing on lion throne*
Cylinder seal. Mesopotamia. Old Babylonian period, c. 1850–1700
B.C. Hematite. 25 × 14 mm. Toronto, Canada, Lands of the Bible
Archaeology Foundation, The Royal Ontario Museum. Photograph:
David A. Loggie.

The goddess Inanna/Ishtar stands upon a dais formed of two of
her lions, back to back. She gazes serenely out at the viewer, wearing
her flounced robe and multiple-horned miter. A weapon composed
of a mace flanked by two curved blades surmounted by decorative
lion-head finials is held in her outstretched right hand. An anonymous
goddess raises her hands in supplication to the magnificent Inanna.

101   *Lovers with Tambourine and Lyre*
Clay plaque showing erotic scene. Larsa, Mesopotamia. Isin-Larsa–
Old Babylonian period, c. 2000–1600 B.C. Beige clay. 8.0 × 6.5 cm.
Paris, Louvre, AO 16924, Barrelet 591

A couple stand back to back, either acrobatically dancing, making love, or possibly both. The male figure turns to look at his partner
while playing a lyre held to his chest. As she looks back at her

companion, the woman shakes a tambourine, her long hair cascading behind her upraised arm.

Erotic content is evident in all aspects of this scene: in the sexual posturing of the nude male and long-haired female, in their dancelike movements, and in their musical instruments. As noted by Ann Draffkorn Kilmer, allusions to the tautness of the strings of instruments such as lyres are found in Sumerian and Akkadian love charms to ensure potency.

Tambourines are usually held by nude female figures and, in one instance, on a cylinder seal from Mari, by the goddess Ishtar/Inanna. Accordingly, the instrument is associated with sexual love, with seduction, and perhaps with the cult of the goddess. Thus the two figures seen here are not secular performers, but provide joyful music and erotic dancing as an accompaniment to and celebration of a cult ritual, perhaps the sacred marriage.

5. *Lady of the Morning*

102   *Inanna with Date Palm and* Anzu-*bird*
       Cylinder seal. Mesopotamia. Neo-Sumerian period, c. 2112–2004
       B.C. Steatite. 27 × 14 mm. Toronto, Canada, Lands of the Bible
       Archaeology Foundation, The Royal Ontario Museum

On this seal, Inanna raises her hand in greeting to the worshippers who approach her while she looks "in sweet wonder from heaven" directly out at the viewer. Above her hand is an eagle, perhaps the lion-headed *Anzu*. Before her in the field is a date palm within a vessel, the focus of ritual libations before the goddess in other scenes. Beneath her feet lies her lion. An elaborate throne supports her. Empowered by her date palm and the *Anzu*-bird, Inanna is better able to rule and judge wisely for her people.

Human worshippers frequently petition deities in scenes and inscriptions on seals; the seal in effect becomes a permanent prayer to the deity. Here a bald, bare-footed worshipper is held by the wrist and led by a suppliant goddess before the awesome Inanna/Ishtar.

The seal's inscription states that it belongs to Lu-igallim, who is the *lumah*-priest of Ninibgal, "Lady of the Big House," probably another name for Inanna. Perhaps it is Lu-igallim who is led by the goddess into Inanna's presence here.

6. *The Lady Who Ascends into the Heavens*

104   *Bringing Gifts to Inanna*

Alabaster vase. Uruk (level III), c. 3100–2900 B.C. h. 3 ft. Iraq Museum. Photograph courtesy of Hirmer Verlag, Munich.

The upper register of this enormous pedestal vase probably shows the goddess Inanna before the twin-doorpost entrance to her temple. A ritually nude figure, perhaps a priest, presents her with a vessel filled with the fruits of the land. Behind the priest stands another figure (partially obliterated by damage to the vessel), wearing the long skirt and elaborate belt of the *en* who assumes the role of groom in the sacred marriage with Inanna. The ceremony may be portrayed here.

(An ancient repair with copper rivets is visible above the head of the goddess, indicating that the vase was treasured in antiquity.)

106   *Inanna Receiving Offering*

Cylinder seal. Late Uruk–Jemdet Nasr period, 3200–3000 B.C. Magnesite. 4.7 × 4.2 cm. Dresden, Staatliche Kunstsammlungen

Although unprovenanced, this cylinder seal bears a scene that is closely related to the one depicted in the upper register of the "Warka Vase" excavated at Uruk. The "figure in the net skirt," perhaps the *en* or priest-king of the city of Uruk, brings offerings to Inanna's temple, symbolized by her two gatepost emblems. The long-horned animal that the priest-king carries is in fact a vessel, with a spout on its back perhaps formed of precious metal. Behind him, a second long-haired assistant figure wearing a short net skirt offers a spouted vessel, perhaps filled with beer. Before Inanna's temple enormous vessels are filled with the produce of the land, the fruit and grains of the farmer, flanked by the meat offerings of the shepherd. The bounty of the land of Sumer is here presented to the goddess Inanna.

7. *The Joy of Sumer*

107   *The Bed*

Clay plaque. Ur. (U 25), Mesopotamia. Isin-Larsa–Old Babylonian period, c. 2000–1600 B.C. Baked clay. London, The British Museum, BM 116506

This clay model of a bed clearly shows the pattern of the basketry "mattress" that was lashed to the wooden frame. Actual beds of this type were found in a cemetery at the site of Mari. Such beds were probably used by individuals of high social status, for the majority of the people of ancient Mesopotamia slept on mats on the floor. Other terracotta beds supporting intertwined couples suggest that such beds were used for ritual purposes, as in the enactment of the sacred marriage.

108   *Lovers Embracing*
Clay plaque. Mesopotamia. Isin-Larsa–Old Babylonian period, c. 2000–1600 B.C. Baked clay. London, The British Museum, BM 113181

This damaged terracotta bed holds roundly modeled male and female figures. As they kiss, each wraps one hand about the partner's neck and the other around the waist, in gestures evocative of deep human emotion. The scene's ritual rather than secular nature is suggested by the baldness of the male figure. Similar shaven heads are believed to characterize priestly or royal figures.

109   *Musician with Upright Harp*

109   *Musician with Horizontal Harp*

Musicians with upright and horizontal harps. Mesopotamia. Ur III–Isin-Larsa period, c. 2100–1800 B.C. Baked clay plaques. 12 × 7 cm.; 7.3 × 8.5 cm, respectively. Paris, Louvre, AO 12453 and AO 12454, respectively. Barrelet 775, 776

Seated on stools, two male figures play harps. The first holds a vertical harp against his shoulder; the second cradles a horizontal harp against his chest and plucks it with a plectrum.

Of the three categories of Sumero-Babylonian instruments—percussion, wind, and strings—the strings are traditionally associated with potency and with the cult that is played before the goddess Inanna and the king in this hymn. Here the harp's sound is said "to drown out the southern storm," providing us with some idea of the loudness of the music it produced. Other texts liken the sound of a stringed instrument, perhaps a lyre, to the thunder of the Storm God, Adad. Bulls—the animal symbol of storm and fertility gods like Adad —actually form the soundbox of lyres excavated at the Royal Cemetery at Ur. The bull thus seemingly emits the thunderous sound of this stringed instrument.

The sacred nature of these musical instruments is suggested by texts which relate that offerings were brought to lyres as to statues of the gods. Accordingly, to play such holy instruments, musicians had first to purify their fingers, perhaps by washing.

In Sumerian music, a development can be traced from a five-note (pentatonic) to a later eight-note (heptatonic) scale, as pointed out by Marcelle Duchesne Guillemin.

111 *Husband and Wife*
Clay plaque. Tello (Girsu), Mesopotamia. Isin-Larsa–Old Babylonian period, c. 2000–1600 B.C. Baked clay. h. 11 cm.; w. 6.4 cm. Paris, Louvre, AO 16676

Fully clothed male and female figures lie gazing intently at each other on a bed; the scored edge of the bed is visible behind the woman. Each wears a padded diadem that may be specifically priestly headgear, according to Madeline Noveck. Their hair has been elaborately coiffed into chignons, and in the case of the male figure into a long spiral curl. Each holds one hand at waist level and the other encircling the partner's waist. Both wear garments that wrap obliquely about the body. Multiple necklaces and bracelets adorn the woman.

SOURCES FOR INANNA'S STORIES AND HYMNS

Many Sumerologists contributed to the deciphering of Sumerian grammar and vocabulary. The following notes acknowledge the specific sources used by the authors to create this book.

The *Huluppu*-Tree

Translations of "The *Huluppu*-Tree," which is part of the epic tale "Gilgamesh, Enkidu, and the Nether World," can be found in S. N. Kramer's *The Sumerians: Their History, Culture, and Character* (University of Chicago Press, 1963), pp. 197–205, and in Aaron Shaffer's doctoral dissertation presented to the Oriental Department of the University of Pennsylvania (1963), entitled "Sumerian Sources of Tablet XII of the Epic of Gilgamesh."

Inanna and the God of Wisdom

"Inanna and the World Order" has been edited by Gertrud Farber-Flugge, under the title "Der Mythos 'Inanna und Enki' mit besonderer Berücksichtigung der liste der *me*" (Biblical Institute Press, Rome, 1973). A sketch of its contents, together with translations of several key passages, was first published in Samuel Noah Kramer's *Sumerian Mythology* (3rd ed., University of Pennsylvania Press, 1972), pp. 64–8.

The Courtship of Inanna and Dumuzi

Translations of most of the poems relating to the Inanna-Dumuzi courtship can be found in S. N. Kramer's contribution to the 3rd edition of *Ancient Near Eastern Texts Relating to the Old Testament* (James Pritchard, ed., Princeton

University Press, 1969), pp. 41, 496, 637–45; in his "Cuneiform Studies and the History of Literature" (*Proceedings of the American Philosophical Society,* vol. 107, 1963); and in *The Sacred Marriage Rite* (University of Indiana Press, 1969), pp. 49–106, and *From the Poetry of Sumer* (University of Berkeley Press, 1979), pp. 71–98).

The translation of the phrase "the agate necklace of fertility" was offered to Diane Wolkstein by Miguel Civil of the University of Chicago.

The Descent of Inanna
From the Great Above to the Great Below

Translations of "The Descent of Inanna" can be found in S. N. Kramer's "Inanna's Descent to the Nether World: Continued and Revised" (*Journal of Cuneiform Studies,* vol. 5, 1951, pp. 1–17), *The Sacred Marriage Rite,* pp. 107–33, and the article in a forthcoming volume of the *Proceedings of the American Philosophical Society* entitled "Sumerian Literature and the British Museum"; in William B. Sladek's doctoral dissertation presented to the Department of Near Eastern Studies of the Johns Hopkins University (1974), entitled "Inanna's Descent to the Nether World"; and in Thorkild Jacobsen's *The Treasures of Darkness* (Yale University Press, 1978), pp. 53–63.

The Dream of Dumuzi
A translation of "Dumuzi's Dream" can be found in Bendt Alster's monograph *Dumuzi's Dream* from *Mesopotamia,* I (Copenhagen, 1974), which is based in large part on contributions by Adam Falkenstein, Thorkild Jacobsen, J. J. Van Dijk, and S. N. Kramer. "Dumuzi and Geshtinanna" can be found in Sladek's dissertation.

New translations to be found in "The Descent of Inanna" were generously offered to Diane Wolkstein by Miguel Civil of the University of Chicago. They are "the double strand of beads," "Let the beer of his funeral rite be poured into the cup," "A maid, as tall as heaven . . . waits outside the palace gates," "the small *galla* . . . the size of low picket fences," "a single growing reed trembles for me," "The bottom of my churn drops away," and "The churn lies silent."

The Return
The text of "The Return" is a compilation of several Sumerian lamentations. "The Lady Weeps Bitterly" can be found in S. N. Kramer's *Sacred Marriage Rite* on p. 128 and in Jacobsen's *The Treasures of Darkness* on page 50. Translations of "The Wild Bull Lives No More," "My Heart Plays the Reed Pipe of

Mourning," and "O My Brother! Who Is Your Sister," can be found in *The Treasures of Darkness,* pp. 50, 53–4, 54–5, and 66, respectively.

Seven Hymns to Inanna

Translations of the hymns can be found in David Reisman's doctoral dissertation presented to the Oriental Department of the University of Pennsylvania (1969), entitled "The Sumerian Royal Hymns." The first part of "Loud Thundering Storm" is taken from "Queen of the Earth Gods," in S. N. Kramer's *From the Poetry of Sumer,* p. 89; the second part is taken from Reisman's dissertation.

NOTES ON THE
TEXTUAL EDITING

The following is an account of the specific changes that depart from literal Sumerian texts. These notes are especially intended for the Sumerologist, folklorist, storyteller, and dramatist. The Cycle of Inanna is meant not only to be read silently but "loudly" and performed as theatre, ritual, or opera. As live performances, repetitions are not necessarily tedious; they can be glorious.

The *Huluppu*-Tree

When Inanna speaks to Utu and Gilgamesh, she condenses the first section of the Sumerian text of 13 lines into 5 lines as has been done. However, beginning from line 14 of the first section, "He set sail; the Father set sail," Inanna retells the story both times line by line in the Sumerian text (referring to herself in the third person) until the line, "How Inanna wept!" Wolkstein has condensed Inanna's two retellings to Utu and Gilgamesh from 33 or so lines into 19 lines to quicken the dramatic flow of the reading.

Inanna and the God of Wisdom

The entire list of *me* is recited four times in the original Sumerian story (the complete list, in fourteen groupings, appears on pp. 16–18). The four listings in this text have been modified in the following ways:

The first time the *me* are recited (pp. 14–15), the offerings have been reduced from fourteen groupings to three. Enki's first offering to Inanna corresponds to the first grouping of the complete list of *me*. Enki's second and third offerings have been selected to relate to Inanna's life story.

The second time the *me* are recited (pp. 16–18), the text follows the complete list as given in the Sumerian.

The third time the *me* are recited (pp. 19–20), the groups have again been reduced to three. The first offering corresponds to the first grouping of the complete list of *me*. The second and third offerings were chosen to relate to the drama taking place between Enki and Inanna.

The fourth time the *me* are recited (p. 26), the original Sumerian consists of all the previously given *me* as well as the new *me*. In this text, only the new *me* are given.

The Courtship of Inanna and Dumuzi

To form the section here called "The Courtship of Inanna and Dumuzi," Diane Wolkstein selected among the different love songs scattered in museums throughout the world. Samuel Noah Kramer deciphered them, and Wolkstein then retranslated and ordered them so that the story would lead from the personal romance of the young lovers to the more public ritual of the king and queen in the sacred marriage rite. The rosettes indicate breaks between the different pieces of the courtship texts.

The Descent of Inanna

Several compositions are combined to form "The Descent of Inanna." The first section, "From the Great Above to the Great Below," follows the Sumerian text until there is a break on line 381 of twenty lines that are not yet completely decipherable. Here our first section ends at the break in the text.

"The Dream of Dumuzi" is composed of Alster's "Dumuzi's Dream" and sections from the more fragmentary "Dumuzi and Geshtinanna" story.

"The Return" is composed of several mourning songs and then, with the appearance of Geshtinanna, of Kramer's tentative translation of the last fifteen lines of "From the Great Above to the Great Below."

From the Great Above to the Great Below

In the Sumerian text, Inanna repeats three times to Ninshubur the plea she wishes her to deliver to Enlil, Nanna, and Enki. The exact speech is given on p. 54, after which "Weep before Nanna" . . . "Weep before Enki" is used rather than repeating the entire plea.

To prolong the comic relief on pp. 65–66, Sladek's translation of "belly–back" and Jacobsen's translation "heart–liver" have been added to Kramer's translation of "inside–outside."

The Dream of Dumuzi

On p. 78, after the speech "Let your dogs devour us," there occurs a section of about fifteen lines that is not clearly understandable. At this point a section from "Dumuzi and Geshtinanna" has been substituted. Wolkstein returns to the text of "The Dream of Dumuzi" with the line: "The *galla* went to Dumuzi's friend" on p. 80.

On p. 83, after Geshtinanna's grief "covered the horizon," five *galla* enter the sheepfold, and Dumuzi and the sheepfold are destroyed. The seven *galla* section from "Dumuzi and Geshtinanna" is substituted. Wolkstein then concludes with the last three lines from "The Dream of Dumuzi."

The Return

The lamentations have been edited to accord with the epithets and place names already used in the text.

Seven Hymns to Inanna

The Seven Hymns to Inanna follow Reisman's translations of Iddin-Dagan's Hymns to Inanna. To the second hymn has been added parts of the Ishme-Dagan Hymn to Inanna from the same period, 1900 B.C. Since the two hymns have the similar contents of the monthly worship of Inanna by the gods and people of Sumer, it seemed important to add Inanna's raging, stormy aspects in order to form the full view that the Sumerian poets present of their passionate, fructifying, yet terrifying and unfathomable Goddess of Love.

SELECTED BIBLIOGRAPHY

Adams, Robert McC. *The Evolution of Urban Society in Early Mesopotamia and Prehispanic Mexico*. Chicago: Aldine Publishing Co., 1966.

Alster, Bendt. "Dumuzi's Dream," *Mesopotamia*, I. Copenhagen, 1974.

Amiet, Pierre. *La Glyptique Mésopotamienne archaique*. Paris, 1961.

————. "The Mythological Repertory in Cylinder Seals of the Agade Period (c. 2335–2155 B.C.)," *Ancient Art in Seals*, ed. Edith Porada. Princeton, N.J.: Princeton University Press, 1980.

Andrae, Walter. *Das Gotteshaus und die Urformen des Bauen im alten Orient*. Berlin, 1930.

————. *Die Ionische Säule*. Berlin, 1933.

Barrelet, Marie-Thérèse. "Les Déesses armées et ailées," *Syria* 32 (1955), pp. 222–60.

————. *Figurines et reliefs en terre cuite de la Mésopotamie antique*, I. Paris: Librairie Orientaliste Paul Geuthner, 1968.

Berlin, Adele. *Enmerkar and Ensuhkesdanna*. Philadelphia: The University Museum, 1979.

Conteneau, Georges. *Everyday Life in Babylon and Assyria*. New York: W. W. Norton, 1966.

Duchesne-Guillemin, Marcelle. "Appendix: Note complémentaire sur la découverte de la gamme babylonienne," *Studies in Honor of Benno Landsberger* (Assyriological Studies 16). Chicago, 1965, pp. 268–72.

Edzard, Dietz Otto. "The Early Dynastic Period," *The Near East: The Early Civilizations*, eds. Jean Bottero, Elena Cassin and Jean Vercoutter. New York: Delacorte Press, 1967, pp. 52–90.

Eliade, Mircea. *Myths, Dreams, and Mysteries*. London: Harvill Press, 1960.

————. *Myth and Reality*. New York: Harper & Row, 1963.

Falkenstein, Adam. *Archaische Texte aus Uruk*. Ausgrabungen der Deutschen Forschungsgemeinschafte in Uruk-Warka, II. Leipzig, Germany, 1936.

————. "The Prehistory and Protohistory of Western Asia," *The Near East:*

The Early Civilizations, eds. Jean Bottero, Elena Cassin and Jean Vercoutter. New York: Delacorte Press, 1967, pp. 1–51.

Falkenstein, Adam, and W. von Soden. *Sumerische und akkadische Hymnen und Gebete.* Munich: Artemis Verlag, 1953.

Farkas, Ann. *Prehistoric Uruk.* M.A. thesis, Faculty of Art History and Archaeology, Columbia University.

Frankfort, Henri. *The Art and Architecture of the Ancient Orient.* Baltimore, Md.: Penguin Books, 1955.

———. *Cylinder Seals: A Documentary Essay on the Art and Religion of the Ancient Near East.* London: Macmillan and Co., 1939.

———. "Notes on the Cretan Griffin," *Annual of the British School at Athens,* 37 (1940), pp. 110–22.

Gadd, Cyril J. *Ideas of Divine Rule in the Ancient Near East.* London: Oxford University Press, 1948.

Green, Margaret Whitney. *Eridu in Sumerian Literature.* Ph.D. thesis, Department of Near Eastern Languages, University of Chicago, 1975.

Hallo, W. W., and J. J. A. van Dijk. *The Exaltation of Inanna.* New Haven, 1968.

Heidel, Alexander. *The Gilgamesh Epic and Old Testament Parallels.* Chicago and London: University of Chicago Press, 1963.

Jacobsen, Thorkild. *Toward the Image of Tammuz and Other Essays on Mesopotamian Religion,* ed. William L. Moran. Cambridge, Mass.: Harvard University Press, 1970.

———. *The Treasures of Darkness: A History of Mesopotamian Religion.* New Haven and London: Yale University Press, 1976.

Kilmer, Ann Draffkorn. "The Strings of Musical Instruments: Their Names, Numbers and Significance," *Studies in Honor of Benno Landsberger* (Assyriological Studies 16). Chicago, 1965, pp. 261–68.

Kirk, G. S. *Myth: Its Meaning and Functions in Ancient and Other Cultures* (Sather Classical Lecture: No. 40). Berkeley: University of California Press, 1970.

Kramer, Samuel Noah. "Cuneiform Studies and the History of Literature," *Proceedings of the American Philosophical Society* 107, 1963.

———. *From the Poetry of Sumer: Creation, Glorification, Adoration.* Berkeley, Los Angeles, and London: University of California Press, 1979.

———. *The Sacred Marriage Rite.* Bloomington: University of Indiana Press, 1969.

———. *Sumerian Mythology,* 3d ed. Philadelphia: University of Pennsylvania Press, 1972.

———. *The Sumerians: Their History, Culture, and Character.* Chicago: University of Chicago Press, 1963.

Kristensen, Brede W. *The Meaning of Religion*. Martinus Nijhoff, The Hague, 1960.

Lenzen, Heinrich. "New Discoveries at Warka in Southern Iraq," *Archaeology* 17:2 (1964), pp. 122–31.

————. "Die Architektur in Eanna in der Uruk IV Periode," *Iraq* 36 (1974), pp. 111–28.

Moortgat, Anton. *The Art of Ancient Mesopotamia*. London: Phaidon, 1969.

Noveck, Madeline. "Horned Headdress," *Ladders to Heaven: Art Treasures from the Lands of the Bible*, ed. Oscar White Muscarella. Toronto: McClelland and Steward, 1981 (no. 47), pp. 90–92.

Opificius, Ruth. *Das altbabylonische Terrakottarelief*. Berlin: De Gruyter, 1961.

Oppenheim, A. Leo. *Ancient Mesopotamia: Portrait of a Dead Civilization*. Chicago: University of Chicago Press, 1964.

Orthmann, W., ed. *Der Alte Orient*. Propyläen Kunstgeschichte, Band 14, Propyläen Verlag. Frankfurt am Main: Verlag Ullstein GmbH, 1975.

Parrot, André. *Sumer*. New York: Golden Press, 1961.

Pereira, Sylvia. *Descent to the Goddess*. New York: Inner City Books, 1981.

Porada, Edith, in collaboration with Briggs Buchanan. *Corpus of Ancient Near Eastern Seals in North American Collections I: The Collection of the Pierpont Morgan Library*, Bollingen Series 14. Washington, D.C., 1948.

————. "Sumerian Art in Miniature," *The Legacy of Sumer*, ed. D. Schmandt-Besserat, Bibliotheca Mesopotamica 4. Malibu, Calif.: Undena Publications, 1976, pp. 112–16.

Pritchard, James B., *Ancient Near Eastern Texts Relating to the Old Testament*, 3d ed. Princeton, N.J.: Princeton University Press, 1969.

Reisman, David. *The Sumerian Royal Hymns*. Ph.D. thesis, Oriental Department, University of Pennsylvania, 1969.

Rimmer, Joan. *Ancient Musical Instruments of Western Asia in the Department of Western Asiatic Antiquities, the British Museum*. London: The Trustees of the British Museum, 1969.

Röhmer, W. H. Ph. "Religion of Ancient Mesopotamia," *Historia Religionum: Handbook for the History of Religions*, Vol. I, *Religions of the Past*, ed. C. J. Bleeker and G. Widengren. Leiden: E. J. Brill, 1969.

Schmandt-Besserat. *The Legacy of Sumer*. Malibu, Calif.: Undena Publications, 1976.

Shaffer, Aaron. *Sumerian Sources of Tablet XII of the Epic of Gilgamesh*. Ph.D. thesis, Oriental Department, University of Pennsylvania, 1963.

Sladek, William. *Inanna's Descent to the Nether World*. Ph.D. thesis, Department of Near Eastern Studies, Johns Hopkins University, 1974.

Spyckett, Agnés. "La déesse Lama," *Révue d'assyriologie et d'archaeologie orientale* 54 (1960), pp. 73–84.

211

_____. *Les statues de culte dans les textes Mésopotamiens des origines à la 1re dynastie de Babylone,* Cahiers de la Revue Biblique, 9. Paris, 1968.

Strommenger, Eva, and Max Hirmer. *Cinq millénaires d'art Mésopotamien de 5000 avant Jesus-Christ à Alezandre le Grand,* trans. M. Duval-Valetin Paris: Flammarion, 1964.

_____. "Modele de lit," *Trésors du Musée de Bagdad: 7000 ans d'histoire Mésopotamienne.* Mainz am Rhein: Phillipp von Zabern, 1977 (no. 114).

Van Buren, Elizabeth Douglas. *Symbols of the Gods in Mesopotamian Art, Analecta Orientalia* 23. Rome: Pontificum Institutum Biblicum, 1945.

_____. "The Rain Goddess as Represented in Early Mesopotamia," *Analecta Biblica* 12 (1959), pp. 343–55.

_____. "Religious Rites and Rituals in the Time of Uruk IV–III," *Archiv für Orientforschung* 30 (1939–41), pp. 32–45.

_____. "The Rosette in Mesopotamian Art," *Zeitschrift für Assyriologie* NF XI (XLV) (1939), pp. 99–107.

Wooley, C. Leonard. *Excavations at Ur.* London: Ernest Benn, 1954.

ACKNOWLEDGMENTS

I wish to thank my friends and family who stood by me during the three years I was living 5,000 years ago in the service of the Goddess.

My first thanks go to Benjamin Zucker. Our mutual interest in ancient history led us fifteen years ago to read the incredible Sumerian text of "The Lamentations of Ur" and to become admirers of Samuel Noah Kramer. Since then I often spoke to him about the absence of the great heroine in ancient history; to this, he always responded: "You must find her and write about her yourself."

Samuel Noah Kramer's patient and searching scholarship served as a model for me in my construction of the text.

Erlo Van Waveren and Charles Mee were the first of my friends to recognize the importance of the Inanna text. My discussions with each of them clarified many sections of the text and led me to the writing of the commentaries.

My very special thanks to Jinx Roosevelt who assiduously, wisely, and lovingly read and re-read, edited and re-edited the numerous versions of text and commentary. She would smile each time I would show her another *"last"* version of the commentaries.

Elizabeth Williams-Forte was an invaluable help. She listened to my many queries on the problematic aspects of Sumerian culture and always provided just the right article or book.

The questions and suggestions of other friends greatly enriched the book. My thanks to Peter and Lorraine Ackerman, Doris Alberecht of the Jung Library, Olivier Bernier, Robert Bly, Ira Friedlander, Brooke Goffstein, Philip and Phylis Morrison, David Outerbridge, Corethia Qualls, and Gary Wolkstein.

No one could ask for a more supportive and wonderful editor than Hugh Van Dusen at Harper & Row. I am also especially grateful to the care and diligence of Janet Goldstein in the editorial department and Coral Tysliava of the copyediting department at Harper & Row.

Miguel Civil at the University of Chicago gave most generously of his time by reading the text and commentaries and offering the latest Sumerian scholarship for the text.

Whenever I came to an impasse in the text or commentaries, my daughter, Rachel Cloudstone Zucker, would say, "Just say what you mean." I'm still trying.

DIANE WOLKSTEIN

213

SELECTED PRONUNCIATION GUIDE

This selected list of frequently occurring Sumerian words has been chosen to serve as a guide to pronouncing Sumerian words appearing in the stories and hymns of Inanna.

Sumerian syllables are evenly accented, with a light stress occurring on certain syllables according to the word. In two-syllable words, the stress occurs on the first syllable; in four-syllable words, the stress occurs on the third syllable; in three-syllable words, the stress varies between the first and second syllable.

"a" is pronounced *ah*   as in "father"
"e" is pronounced *eh**   as in "bend"
"i" is pronounced *ee*   as in "knee"
"u" is pronounced *oo*   as in "moon"

Inanna   Ee-nah'-nah
Dumuzi   Doo'-moo-zee
Enki   Ehn'-kee
Ereshkigal   Eh-resh-kee'-gahl
Geshtinanna   Gesh-tee-nah'-nah
Gilgamesh   Geel'-gah-mesh
Ninshubur   Neen-shoo'-boor
Utu   Oo'-too

Eridu   Eh'-ree-doo
Uruk   Oo'-rook

abzu   ahb'-zoo
galatur   gah'-lah-toor
galla   gah'-lah
huluppu   hoo-loo'-poo
kur   koor
kurgarra   koor-gah'-rah
*me   may (an exception to the rule)
sukkal   soo'-kahl

INDEX

Italicized page numbers refer to the actual stories and hymns of Inanna.

225

Shara (Inanna's son), x, 70, 161
sheep and sheepfold, v (illus.), 35
    (illus.), 85 (illus.), 177–78,
    185, 192–93
  in "The Courtship of Inanna and
    Dumuzi," 40
  in "The Descent of Inanna," 76,
    77, 83, 84, 86, 167
  in "Inanna and the God of
    Wisdom," 12, 18, 146
shepherd, 35 (illus.), 85 (illus.),
    185, 192–93
  in "The Courtship of Inanna and
    Dumuzi," 31, 33–35, 44–46,
    151, 155
  in "The Descent of Inanna,"
    74–75, 86
  in "Inanna and the God of
    Wisdom," 12
  See also Dumuzi
Shrine, 55 (illus.), 190
  of Enki, see Abzu
  of Inanna, see Eanna
  See also temple architecture
shugurra (crown of the steppe), 12,
    53, 56, 57, 146
Shulgi (son of Ur-Nammu), 118
silver, 54, 61, 62, 157
Sippar, xii
Sirtur, (Ninsun: Sheep Goddess),
    xi, 34, 74, 86–87, 163
sister-brother couples, 166, 167
Sjoberg, Ake, 132
Sladek, William, 132, 201, 206
slavery in Sumer, 120
snakes and serpents, 3 (illus.), 5
    (illus.), 7 (illus.), 178–80
  in "The Descent of Inanna,"
    72–73, 131
  in "The Huluppu-Tree," 6–9,
    137, 141–43, 145, 165
songs, see music and song
stars, see rosettes; Venus
sukkal (servant), 149
  See also Isimud; Neti; Ninshubur

Sumer (Sumerians)
  arts in, 119, 121–22, 136, 137,
    174–77; see also music and
    song
  culture of, 119–25, 169–70
  end of, 126
  geography of, 119
  history of, 115–19
  houses in, 121, 188, 198
  kingship in, 116, 151, 188
  literature of, xiii, 125–26, 136,
    137
  map of, xii
  religion of, ix, 122–25, 171–
    73
  temple architecture of, 119,
    174–75, 188
Sumerian language, xviii, 116
  pronunciation guide for, 216
Susa, xii

tablets, see clay tablets
talents, 9, 143
Tallon, François, 176
Taurus planet (Bull of Heaven),
    157
temple architecture, 119, 174–75,
    188
Thomas, Dylan, 155n., 167n.
Throne, 3 (illus.), 14–15 (illus.),
    178, 182
  of Dumuzi, 71, 162
  of Enki, 13 (illus.), 14, 16, 63
    (illus.), 181, 191
  of Ereshkigal, 45, 46
  of Inanna, 5–9, 52 (illus.), 96,
    98 (illus.), 99, 100 (illus.),
    102 (illus.), 141, 142, 144–46,
    189, 195, 196
  of Ningal and Nanna, 9 (illus.),
    180–81
  sacred marriage, 31, 107, 109
Tigris River, xii, 47, 147, 181
Tolstoy, Leo, 156
tree(s), 5 (illus.), 40 (illus.) 46,